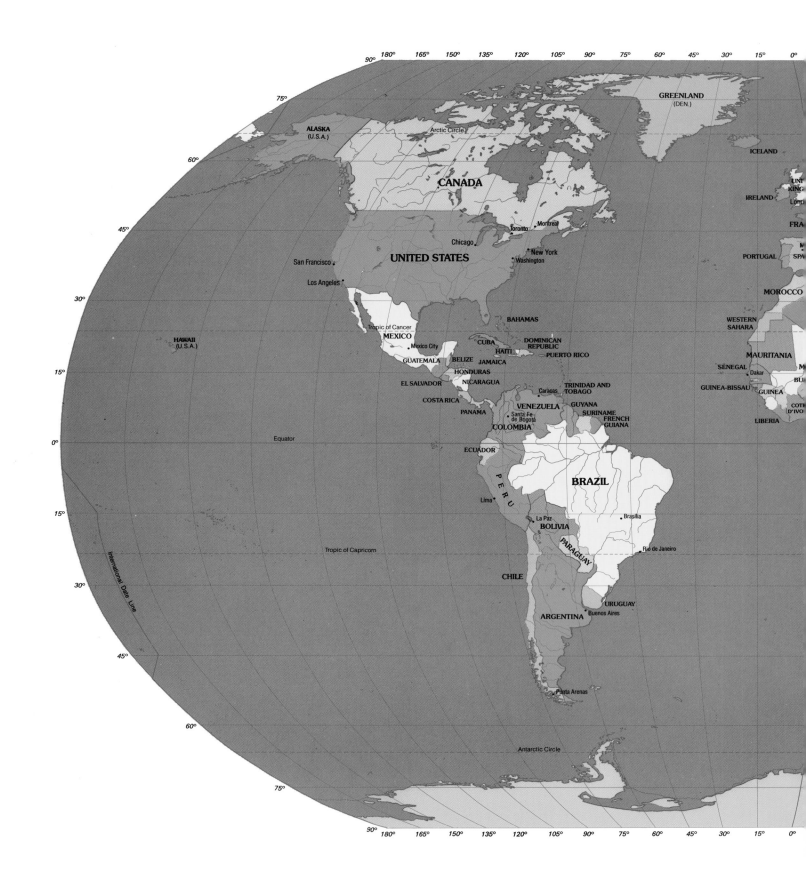

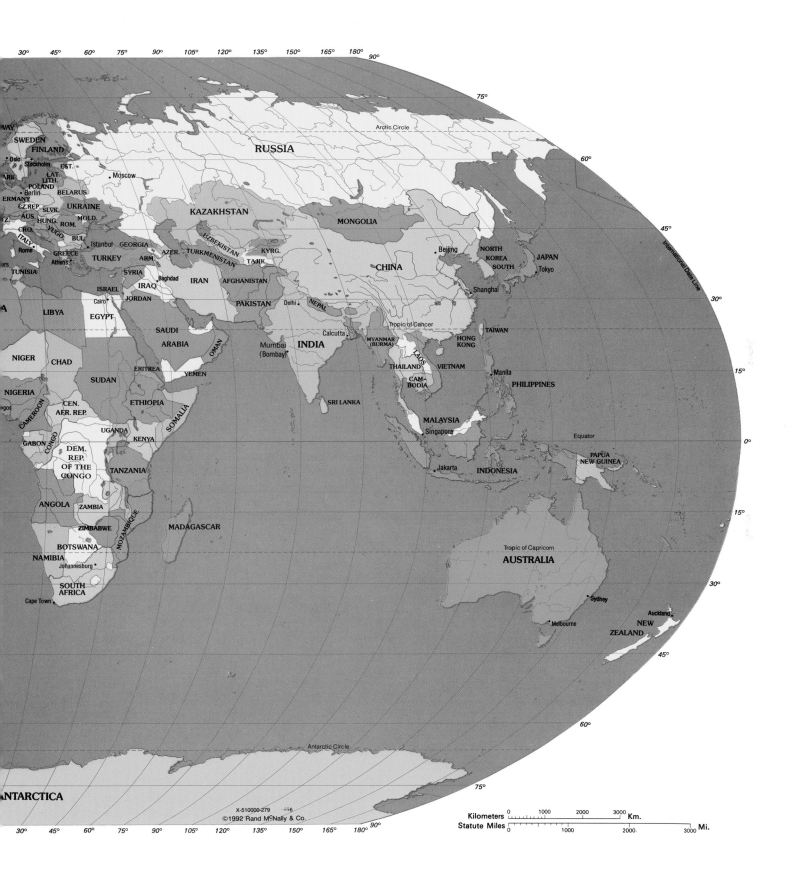

30° 45° 60° 75° 90° 105° 120° 135° 150° 165° 180° 90°

75°

Arctic Circle

NORWAY
SWEDEN
FINLAND
• Oslo
• Stockholm EST.
ARK LAT.
LITH.
POLAND
GERMANY • Berlin BELARUS
CZ.REP. SLVK. **UKRAINE**
AUS. HUNG. ROM. MOLD.
CRO. YUGO. BUL.
ITALY
Rome GREECE Istanbul **GEORGIA**
Athens **TURKEY** ARM. AZER.
TUNISIA

RUSSIA

• Moscow

60°

KAZAKHSTAN

MONGOLIA

45°

UZBEKISTAN
KYRG.
TURKMENISTAN TAJIK.

CHINA

• Beijing

**NORTH
KOREA**
SOUTH **JAPAN**
• Tokyo

SYRIA
Baghdad **IRAN**
ISRAEL **IRAQ**
JORDAN
Cairo

AFGHANISTAN

Shanghai •

30°

LIBYA
EGYPT

PAKISTAN

Delhi • **NEPAL**

Tropic of Cancer

TAIWAN

**SAUDI
ARABIA**

Calcutta

**HONG
KONG**

Mumbai
(Bombay) • **INDIA**

MYANMAR
(BURMA)
LAOS

15°

NIGER
CHAD

ERITREA
YEMEN

THAILAND
CAM-
BODIA
VIETNAM

Manila •

OMAN

PHILIPPINES

NIGERIA
SUDAN

ETHIOPIA

SRI LANKA

CEN.
AFR. REP.

CAMEROON
MALAYSIA
Singapore

Equator

0°

GABON CONGO
UGANDA
**DEM.
REP.
OF THE
CONGO**
KENYA

SOMALIA

Jakarta •
INDONESIA

**PAPUA
NEW GUINEA**

TANZANIA

15°

ANGOLA
ZAMBIA

MOZAMBIQUE

MADAGASCAR

ZIMBABWE

BOTSWANA
Tropic of Capricorn

AUSTRALIA

NAMIBIA
Johannesburg •

30°

**SOUTH
AFRICA**

Sydney •

Auckland •

Cape Town •

Melbourne •
**NEW
ZEALAND**

45°

60°

Antarctic Circle

ANTARCTICA

75°

International Date Line

X-510000-279 446
©1992 Rand McNally & Co.

30° 45° 60° 75° 90° 105° 120° 135° 150° 165° 180° 90°

Kilometers 0 1000 2000 3000 Km.
Statute Miles 0 1000 2000 3000 Mi.

Rand McNally
Children's Atlas of the
United States

Washington, D.C., is the capital of the United States. The letters *D* and *C* stand for "District of Columbia," which is where the city of Washington is situated. The district is a piece of land owned by the government that has an area of 63 square miles (163 sq. km.) and a population of 609,909. It is not a part of any state, but is surrounded on three sides by Maryland, with the fourth side formed by the Potomac River. Shown here is the Capitol building in Washington, which houses the legislative branch of the federal government.

Contents

United States _____ 8

Alabama _____ 10

Alaska _____ 12

Arizona _____ 14

Arkansas _____ 16

California _____ 18

Colorado _____ 20

Connecticut _____ 22

Delaware _____ 24

Florida _____ 26

Georgia _____ 28

Hawaii _____ 30

Idaho _____ 32

Illinois _____ 34

Indiana _____ 36

Iowa _____ 38

Kansas _____ 40

Kentucky _____ 42

Louisiana _____ 44

Maine _____ 46

Maryland _____ 48

Massachusetts _____ 50

Michigan _____ 52

Minnesota _____ 54

Mississippi _____ 56

Missouri _____ 58

Rand McNally Children's Atlas of the United States

General manager: Russell L. Voisin
Managing editor: Jon M. Leverenz
Editor, writer: Elizabeth Fagan Adelman
Cartographic editor: V. Patrick Healy
Art director: Bill Pieper
Production editor: Laura C. Schmidt
Production manager: John R. Potratz

Rand McNally Children's Atlas of the United States
Copyright © 1994, 1989 by Rand McNally & Company
Revised Printing, 1996
Published and printed in the United States of America

Photographs from *Rand McNally's America* copyright © 1989 by Rand McNally & Company, used with permission.
Population data from Market Statistics, S&MM 1994 "Survey of Buying Power." State emblems from Newfield Publications Inc.

00 99 98 97

Library of Congress Cataloging-in-Publication Data

Rand McNally and Company.
    Children's atlas of the United States. -- Rev. ed.

        p.   cm.
    Includes index.
    ISBN 0-528-83362-6
    ISBN 0-528-83540-8 (pbk.)
    1. United States -- Maps for children.
    [1. United States -- Maps.   2. Atlases.]
1. Title.
G1201.R344   1993   < G&M >
912.73--dc20
                                        93-40197
                                        CIP
                                        MAP AC

Printed on recycled paper.

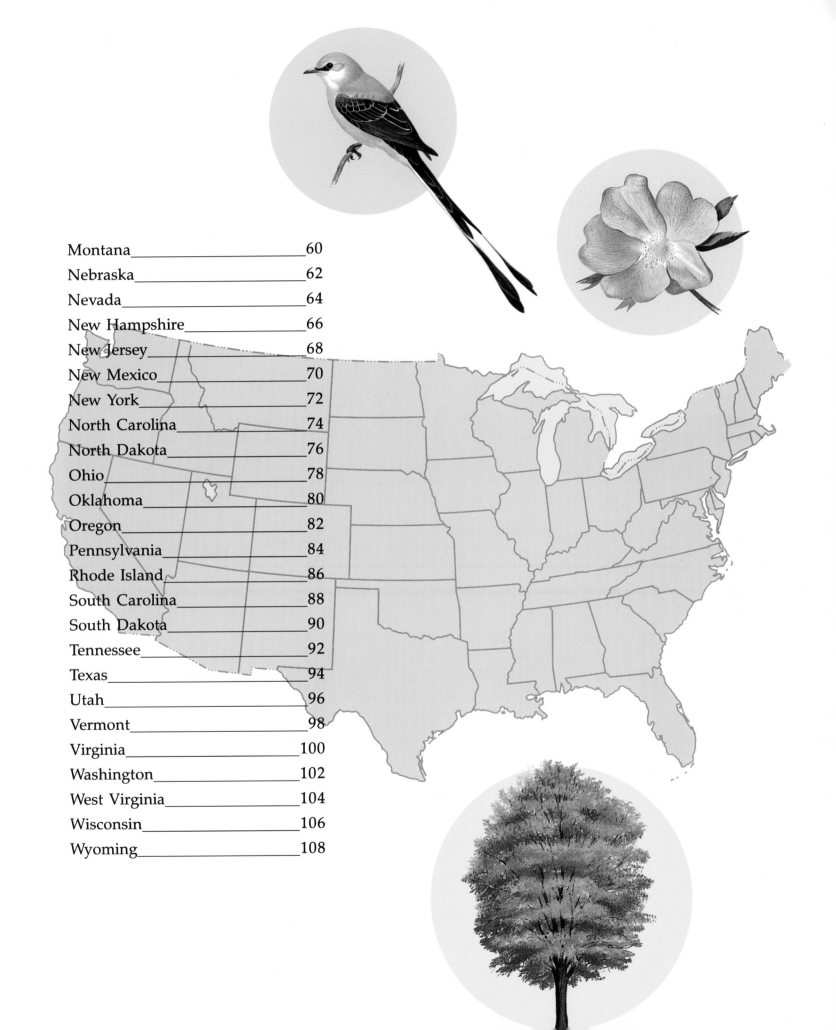

Montana	60
Nebraska	62
Nevada	64
New Hampshire	66
New Jersey	68
New Mexico	70
New York	72
North Carolina	74
North Dakota	76
Ohio	78
Oklahoma	80
Oregon	82
Pennsylvania	84
Rhode Island	86
South Carolina	88
South Dakota	90
Tennessee	92
Texas	94
Utah	96
Vermont	98
Virginia	100
Washington	102
West Virginia	104
Wisconsin	106
Wyoming	108

This map shows the United States and its major geographical features, state capitals, and other metropolitan centers. The area of the United States is 3,539,341 square miles (9,166,851 sq. km.) and its population is 248,709,873.

Scale 1:12,600,000; one inch to 200 miles Polyconic Projection

95° 90° 85° 80° 75° 70° 65°

50°

C A N A D A

LAKE SUPERIOR

MINNESOTA

St. Paul
Minneapolis

WISCONSIN

Madison
Milwaukee

Chicago

IOWA

Des Moines

Springfield

Kansas City

St. Louis
Jefferson City

MISSOURI

Topeka

ILLINOIS

INDIANA

Indianapolis

MICHIGAN

LAKE MICHIGAN

Lansing
Detroit

LAKE HURON

LAKE ONTARIO
Buffalo

LAKE ERIE

Cleveland

OHIO

Columbus

Cincinnati

Frankfort

KENTUCKY

Ohio

NEW YORK
Albany

Montpelier
VT. N.H.
Concord

MAINE
Augusta

M O U N T A I N S

MASS. Boston
Hartford Providence
CONN. R.I.

N.J. New York
Trenton
Philadelphia

PENNSYLVANIA
Harrisburg

Pittsburgh

Baltimore
MD. Dover
Annapolis DEL.

Washington
D.C.

Richmond

40°

WEST
VIRGINIA

Charleston

Nashville

TENNESSEE

VIRGINIA

Raleigh

NORTH CAROLINA

35°

ARKANSAS

Little Rock

MISSISSIPPI

Jackson

A P P A L A C H I A N

Atlanta

ALABAMA

Montgomery

Columbia
SOUTH
CAROLINA

GEORGIA

30°

LOUISIANA

Baton
Rouge

New Orleans

Houston

F L O R I D A

Tallahassee

GULF OF MEXICO

Mississippi

A T L A N T I C   O C E A N

BAHAMAS

Miami

25°

95° 90°
Longitude West of Greenwich

85° 80° 75°

0 25 50 75 100 200 300 400 500 Miles
0 100 200 400 600 800 Kilometers

National capital ⊛
State capital ★ Urban area

40,000 SQ MI
AREA
0 100 200
Miles

Alabama

Alabama's natural resources are found not only in its land but also in its waters. Like many other Gulf Coast states, Alabama contains offshore natural gas deposits. Here, drilling for natural gas takes place off of Mobile Bay, near the Gulf of Mexico.

Russell Cave National Monument, near Bridgeport, shows the remains of several prehistoric cultures. The cave is believed to have been inhabited continuously from 7000 B.C. to 1000 A.D. Visitors can see exhibits that show different aspects of life in ancient times.

In the 1950s and 1960s, the rest of the country watched Alabama closely. During these decades, Martin Luther King, Jr. and other people led civil rights protests in Alabama. These protests helped bring an end to racial segregation across the country. Like other states in the South, Alabama was once a land of prosperous cotton plantations, and the state fought on the Confederate side in the Civil War.

Many Alabamians have jobs in manufacturing. Iron and steel are significant products. Farmers still raise cotton, but livestock and dairy products are more important today.

Beaches along the Gulf Coast bring vacationers. They also come to the state's historic sites, which include restored plantations with beautiful gardens.

Most of Alabama is made up of a low coastal plain. In the northeast, there are some hills and low mountains. The state's climate is humid, with long, hot summers and short, mild winters.

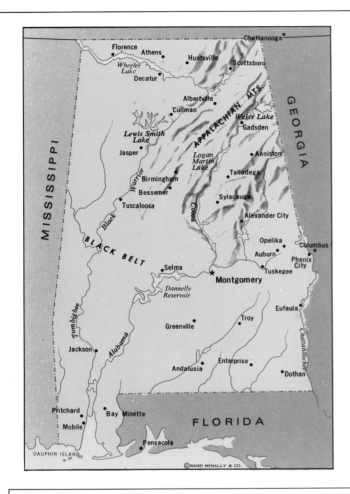

ALABAMA

Capital
Montgomery (195,300 people)

Area
50,750 square miles (131,443 sq. km.)
Rank: 28th

Population
4,200,000 people Rank: 22nd

Statehood
Dec. 14, 1819 (22nd state admitted)

Principal rivers
Alabama River, Tombigbee River

Highest point
Cheaha Mountain; 2,405 feet (733 m.)

Largest city
Birmingham (264,700 people)

Motto
We dare defend our rights

Song
"Alabama"

Famous people
George Washington Carver, Helen Keller

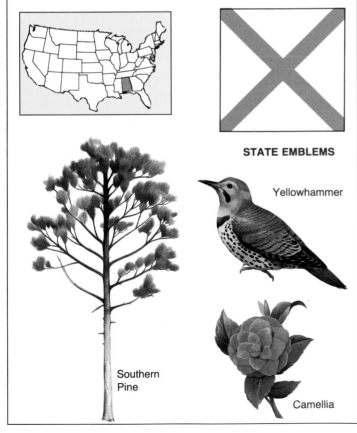

STATE EMBLEMS

Yellowhammer

Southern Pine

Camellia

Many types of spacecraft are on display at the Alabama Space and Rocket Center, near Huntsville.

Alaska

Alaska is a land of extremes. It is the largest state, the northernmost, the westernmost, the most sparsely populated, and it has the nation's highest peak.

Alaska is also a land of spectacular scenery, with many beautiful mountains, glaciers, and huge areas of frozen plain, or *tundra*. The vast national parks and preserves are filled with wildlife, and thousands of tourists visit them every year.

The first Alaskans crossed the Bering Strait about thirty thousand years ago. The United States bought the region from Russia in 1867. In the late 1890s, gold was discovered in Alaska. As a result, many people seeking riches came to the region—in other words, there was a gold rush.

The United States government, especially the armed forces, is Alaska's biggest employer. Drilling for oil and fishing are important activities.

Near the ocean, the climate is milder, but inland, the summers are short and winters are very long and cold.

Sitka, shown here, is one of Alaska's oldest cities. Founded by a Russian in 1799, the city served as the capital of the region until 1900. Sitka's location on the southern arm of Alaska and the Pacific Ocean make it an important port.

In the snowy regions of the world, dogsleds have been an effective mode of transportation for hundreds of years. Today, however, they have been largely replaced by snowmobiles and airplanes. But dogsled races such as the Iditarod are still held in Alaska.

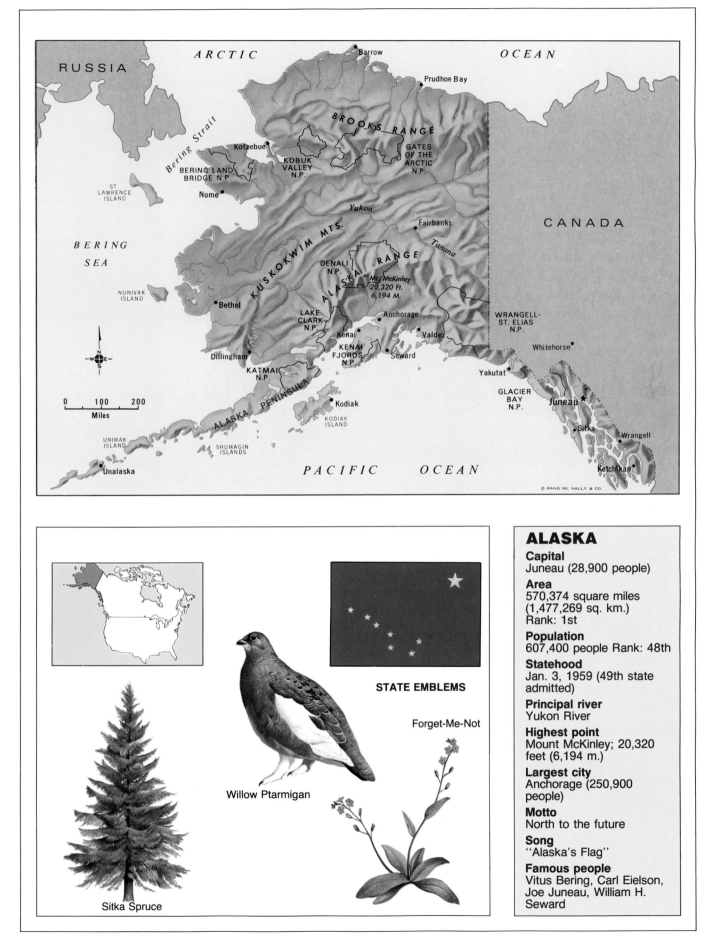

Map labels

RUSSIA

ARCTIC OCEAN

Barrow

Prudhoe Bay

Bering Strait

BROOKS RANGE

Kotzebue

KOBUK VALLEY N.P.

GATES OF THE ARCTIC N.P.

BERING LAND BRIDGE N.P.

Nome

ST. LAWRENCE ISLAND

BERING SEA

Yukon

Fairbanks

Tanana

CANADA

KUSKOKWIM MTS.

DENALI N.P.

ALASKA RANGE

Mt. McKinley 20,320 Ft. 6,194 M.

NUNIVAK ISLAND

Bethel

LAKE CLARK N.P.

Anchorage

WRANGELL-ST. ELIAS N.P.

Kenai

Valdez

Whitehorse

KENAI FJORDS N.P.

Seward

Dillingham

Yakutat

KATMAI N.P.

GLACIER BAY N.P.

Juneau ★

ALASKA PENINSULA

Kodiak

Sitka

Wrangell

KODIAK ISLAND

UNIMAK ISLAND

SHUMAGIN ISLANDS

PACIFIC OCEAN

Ketchikan

Unalaska

N W E S

0   100   200
Miles

© RAND MC NALLY & CO.

STATE EMBLEMS

Sitka Spruce

Willow Ptarmigan

Forget-Me-Not

ALASKA

Capital
Juneau (28,900 people)

Area
570,374 square miles
(1,477,269 sq. km.)
Rank: 1st

Population
607,400 people Rank: 48th

Statehood
Jan. 3, 1959 (49th state admitted)

Principal river
Yukon River

Highest point
Mount McKinley; 20,320 feet (6,194 m.)

Largest city
Anchorage (250,900 people)

Motto
North to the future

Song
"Alaska's Flag"

Famous people
Vitus Bering, Carl Eielson, Joe Juneau, William H. Seward

Arizona

At Keet Seel, in northeastern Arizona, are found the remains of cliff dwellings built around one thousand years ago by ancestors of the Pueblos. Several families of Indians, the country's earliest settlers, lived, cooked, and worked in such dwellings.

Almost every day is filled with sunshine in Arizona. Although the climate varies with the height of the land, it tends to be hot and dry. The terrain is made up largely of plateaus, canyons, and mountains.

In winter, people visit Arizona because of its warm climate. In spring, sports fans come to watch baseball teams participate in spring training. All year round, people come to the state to see its scenic beauty.

Indians entered Arizona thousands of years ago, and many of their descendants still live in the state. The Spaniards who came in the 1500s found sophisticated Indian cultures. In the late 1800s, Arizona was the site of many bitter battles between Indians and settlers.

Many Arizonans are engaged in manufacturing. Several types of machinery are made. Mining is also important. In recent years, Arizona has attracted people seeking jobs and a good climate. As a result, Arizona's population has grown very rapidly.

Some places in spectacular Grand Canyon National Park, on the Colorado River, are 1 mile (1.6 kilometers) deep, and others are 18 miles (29 kilometers) wide. The rocks exposed in the canyon show over one billion years of the earth's geologic history.

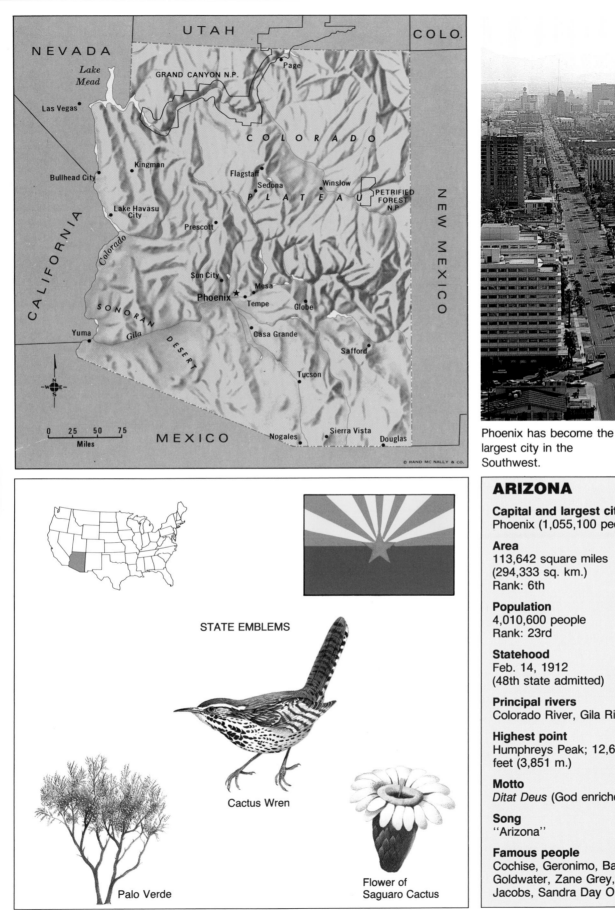

Phoenix has become the largest city in the Southwest.

STATE EMBLEMS

Cactus Wren

Palo Verde

Flower of Saguaro Cactus

ARIZONA

Capital and largest city
Phoenix (1,055,100 people)

Area
113,642 square miles
(294,333 sq. km.)
Rank: 6th

Population
4,010,600 people
Rank: 23rd

Statehood
Feb. 14, 1912
(48th state admitted)

Principal rivers
Colorado River, Gila River

Highest point
Humphreys Peak; 12,633
feet (3,851 m.)

Motto
Ditat Deus (God enriches)

Song
"Arizona"

Famous people
Cochise, Geronimo, Barry
Goldwater, Zane Grey, Helen
Jacobs, Sandra Day O'Connor

Arkansas

Years ago, cotton fields could be seen all over Arkansas. Today, however, rice fields are more common. Because some rice grows best when its roots are underwater, Arkansas's lowlands are well suited for rice. The state grows much of the nation's supply.

Many visitors to Arkansas seek relief from aching joints and tired muscles by bathing in the springs at Hot Springs National Park. Soothing hot mineral water flows from the ground here and is captured and piped into the public baths. Hot Springs is one of the most popular resorts in the United States.

Much of the state is forested, with mountains and rolling hills in the north and west. In the south and east, near the Mississippi River, the terrain is flatter. Long, hot summers and short, mild winters are typical.

Many Arkansans work either in factories or on farms. Processed foods—such as canned goods—are important products, and soybeans and rice are important crops.

The region changed hands among European nations until 1803, when the United States bought it as part of the Louisiana Purchase. In the Civil War, Arkansas sided with the South. The Great Depression of the 1930s affected many, and hundreds of families left the state in search of opportunities.

Buffalo National River, in the Ozarks of northwestern Arkansas, is one of the few unpolluted rivers in the United States. A variety of outdoor activities are available, including canoeing, swimming, fishing, camping, and hiking.

ARKANSAS

Capital and largest city
Little Rock
(179,500 people)

Area
52,075 square miles
(134,874 sq. km.)
Rank: 27th

Population
2,437,400 people
Rank: 33rd

Statehood
June 15, 1836
(25th state admitted)

Principal rivers
Arkansas River,
Mississippi River,
White River

Highest point
Magazine Mountain;
2,753 feet (839 m.)

Motto
Regnat populus (The people rule)

Song
"Arkansas"

Famous people
Hattie Caraway,
Johnny Cash, James
W. Fulbright,
Douglas MacArthur,
James S. McDonnel

STATE EMBLEMS

Pine

Mockingbird

Apple Blossom

A 216-foot (65-meter) tower at Hot Springs.

California

An area that is nicknamed the Silicon Valley extends from San Jose to Redwood City. It is a region that produces much high technology. It is named after the silicon chip, an important part of many electronic devices that are developed here.

Sequoias, or redwoods, are the world's tallest trees. In Redwood National Park are found sequoias that tower more than three hundred feet (ninety meters). Although redwoods are still cut for lumber, efforts are being made to conserve these rare and magnificent trees.

In many ways, California stands alone. It is the most economically productive state in the country. It leads the country in manufacturing and farming. And it has by far the highest population of all the states.

California is one of the country's leading vacation destinations. People come to hike in the several national parks, swim in the Pacific Ocean, and sightsee in the cities. They also come to places like Disneyland and the San Diego Zoo.

California was settled by the Spanish and was part of Mexico when that nation became independent in 1821. In 1848, the United States took control. Californians discovered gold shortly thereafter, and a gold rush was on. As the population increased, so did pressure for statehood.

California is the third largest state in area, after Alaska and Texas. The land features a great central valley and the mountain ranges that surround it. On the coast, there are cool, rainless summers and mild winters. It is hotter farther inland.

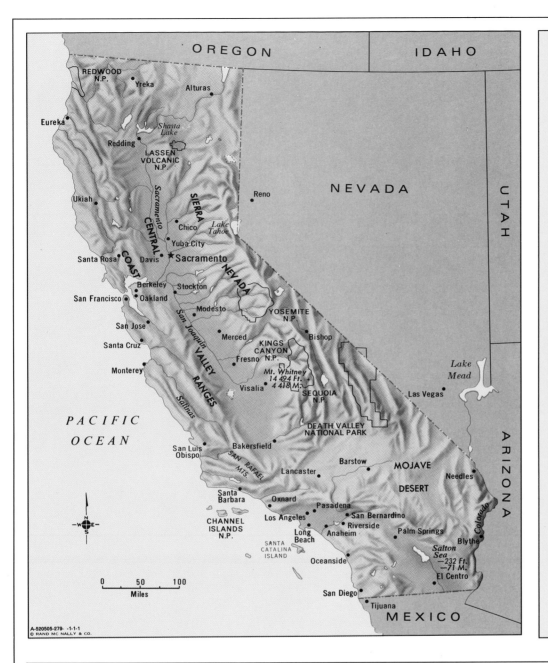

OREGON

IDAHO

REDWOOD N.P.

Yreka

Alturas

Eureka

Shasta Lake

Redding

LASSEN VOLCANIC N.P.

NEVADA

Ukiah

Reno

Sacramento

SIERRA

Chico

Lake Tahoe

Yuba City

Santa Rosa • Davis ★ Sacramento

Berkeley • Stockton

San Francisco • Oakland

Modesto

San Jose

San Joaquin

Santa Cruz

Merced

YOSEMITE N.P.

Bishop

KINGS CANYON N.P.

Fresno

Monterey

VALLEY

Mt. Whitney 14,494 Ft. 4,418 M.

Visalia

SEQUOIA N.P.

Lake Mead

RANGES

Salinas

Las Vegas

PACIFIC OCEAN

San Luis Obispo

Bakersfield

SAN RAFAEL MTS

Lancaster

Barstow

MOJAVE

Needles

DEATH VALLEY NATIONAL PARK

DESERT

Santa Barbara

Oxnard

Pasadena

Los Angeles • San Bernardino

CHANNEL ISLANDS N.P.

Long Beach

Riverside

Anaheim

Palm Springs

SANTA CATALINA ISLAND

Oceanside

Salton Sea −232 Ft. −71 M.

Blythe

El Centro

San Diego

ARIZONA

UTAH

Colorado

Tijuana

MEXICO

N W E S

0   50   100
Miles

A-520505-279- -1-1-1
© RAND MC NALLY & CO.

CALIFORNIA

Capital
Sacramento (391,600 people)

Area
155,973 square miles (403,970 sq. km.)
Rank: 3rd

Population
31,728,200 people
Rank: 1st

Statehood
Sept. 9, 1850 (31st state admitted)

Principal rivers
Colorado River, Sacramento River, San Joaquin River

Highest point
Mount Whitney; 14,494 feet (4,418 m.)

Largest city
Los Angeles (3,495,800 people)

Motto
Eureka (I have found it)

Song
"I Love You, California"

Famous people
Shirley Temple Black, Cesar Chavez, William Randolph Hearst, Marilyn Monroe, Ronald Reagan, Sally Ride, John Steinbeck, Earl Warren

STATE EMBLEMS

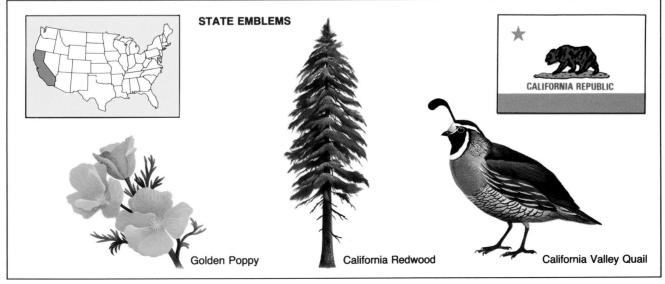

Golden Poppy

California Redwood

CALIFORNIA REPUBLIC

California Valley Quail

Colorado

At the foot of the Sangre de Cristo Mountains, a branch of the Rocky Mountains, lie the Great Sand Dunes. Situated in the southern part of Colorado, the area features some of the largest sand dunes in the country. Sometimes quicksands form in the dunes.

Rocky Mountain National Park is in the heart of some of the nation's best skiing country. The park, which is a wildlife sanctuary, contains a large number of peaks over ten thousand feet and many upland meadows, sheer canyons, and glacial lakes and streams.

A simple fact says much about Colorado's terrain: there are eighty mountain peaks over 14,000 feet (4,267 meters) in the United States, and fifty-three of them are in Colorado. Colorado has the highest average elevation of all the states.

Colorado's beautiful scenery and climate, which features sunny summers and snowy winters, draw visitors who are interested in the outdoors. So do historic sites, which include dinosaur remains, ancient Indian dwellings, and old mining towns.

Some Coloradans make metals, machinery, or food products, while others raise livestock or grow wheat, corn, or hay.

Humans lived in Colorado more than twenty thousand years ago. In the mid 1500s, the first Spanish explorers to come to the region encountered several Indian groups. Eastern Colorado was included in the Louisiana Purchase of 1803; the west was gained from Mexico in 1848. A few years later, gold was discovered, and people flocked to Colorado.

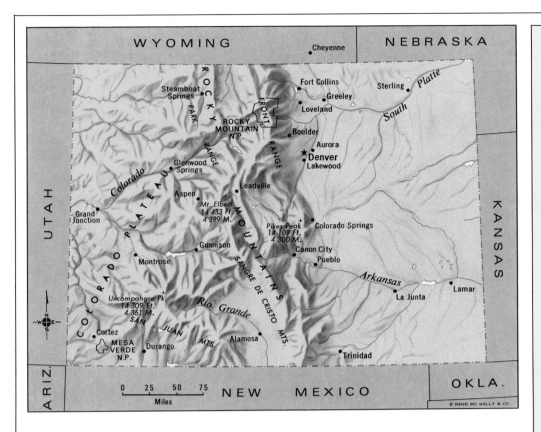

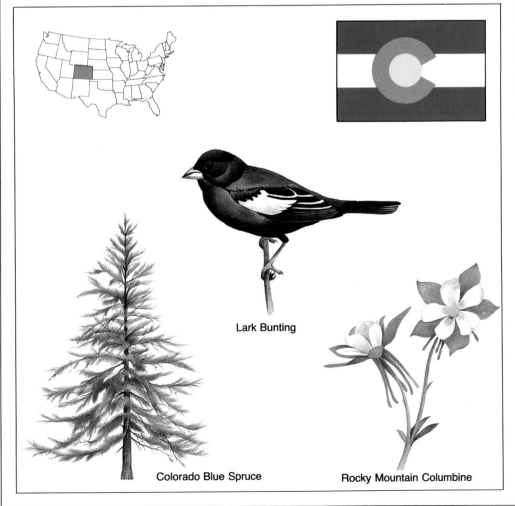

COLORADO

Capital and largest city
Denver (498,000 people)

Area
103,729 square miles (268,658 sq. km.)
Rank: 8th

Population
3,616,000 people
Rank: 26th

Statehood
Aug. 1, 1876
(38th state admitted)

Principal rivers
Arkansas River, Colorado River, South Platte River

Highest point
Mount Elbert; 14,433 feet (4,399 m.)

Motto
Nil sine numine (Nothing without providence)

Song
"Where the Columbines Grow"

Famous people
Frederick Bonfils, M. Scott Carpenter, Douglas Fairbanks, Florence Rena Sabin, Lowell Thomas, Paul Whiteman

Lark Bunting

Colorado Blue Spruce

Rocky Mountain Columbine

Connecticut

The sea has played a major role in Connecticut's history. Mystic Seaport, shown here, is a reconstructed nineteenth-century village where visitors can get a feel for some of that history. Nearby, Mystic Marinelife Aquarium features a wide array of wildlife.

Nathan Hale was a Connecticut school teacher and a famous revolutionary war hero. The British caught him spying and hanged him. Before he died, he declared, "I only regret that I have but one life to lose for my country." Hale's New London schoolhouse is now a museum.

The eastern *megalopolis* is a region of nearly continuous city that stretches from New Hampshire to Virginia. Connecticut, the third smallest state in area, lies nearly at the center of the megalopolis. Despite this location, much of Connecticut is wooded, with rolling hills. The state also has many miles of shoreline. Connecticut's woodlands and beaches attract tourists, and so do the state's historic and cultural sites.

Connecticut has a long history of manufacturing, which today employs about one-third of the work force. Connecticut makes more submarines, helicopters, and jet engines than any other state.

The Dutch came to Connecticut in the early 1600s and discovered several Indian groups. The English soon followed, and some of the towns they founded are among the nation's oldest. Connecticut was one of the thirteen British colonies to fight for independence in the American Revolution.

Winters in Connecticut are cold, and summers are warm.

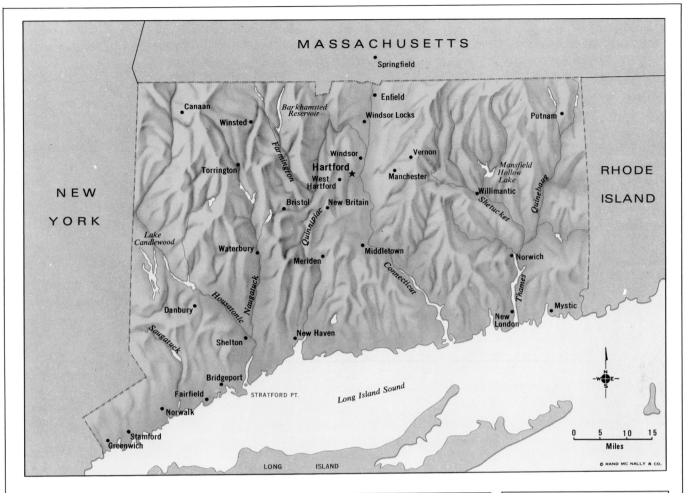

MASSACHUSETTS

Springfield

NEW YORK

Canaan
Winsted
Torrington
Danbury
Shelton
Fairfield
Norwalk
Stamford
Greenwich

Barkhamsted Reservoir
Farmington
Windsor
Hartford
West Hartford
Bristol
New Britain
Waterbury
Meriden
Bridgeport

Enfield
Windsor Locks
Vernon
Manchester
Middletown

Putnam

RHODE ISLAND

Mansfield Hollow Lake
Willimantic
Shetucket
Quinebaug

Norwich
Thames
Mystic
New London

Lake Candlewood
Housatonic
Naugatuck
Saugatuck
Quinnipiac
Connecticut

STRATFORD PT.
Long Island Sound

LONG ISLAND

0 5 10 15
Miles

© RAND MC NALLY & CO.

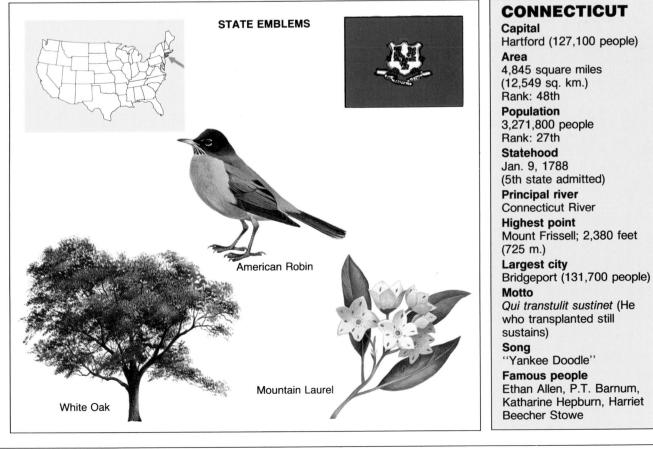

STATE EMBLEMS

American Robin

White Oak

Mountain Laurel

CONNECTICUT

Capital
Hartford (127,100 people)

Area
4,845 square miles
(12,549 sq. km.)
Rank: 48th

Population
3,271,800 people
Rank: 27th

Statehood
Jan. 9, 1788
(5th state admitted)

Principal river
Connecticut River

Highest point
Mount Frissell; 2,380 feet
(725 m.)

Largest city
Bridgeport (131,700 people)

Motto
Qui transtulit sustinet (He
who transplanted still
sustains)

Song
"Yankee Doodle"

Famous people
Ethan Allen, P.T. Barnum,
Katharine Hepburn, Harriet
Beecher Stowe

Delaware

Fishing, sailing, swimming, sunning, biking, and other activities are enjoyed at Rehoboth Beach. Along the beach is a boardwalk with shops and restaurants. Only about two hours from Washington, D.C., Rehoboth Beach is a favorite among the nation's legislators and diplomats.

The chemical industry in Delaware began with a gunpowder mill built by a Frenchman in 1802. Today, the company he started is a huge corporation known as Du Pont, which employs many of the people in Delaware. This chemical plant is typical of many found in the state.

Delaware is sometimes called "the first state." It was one of the thirteen colonies to fight the British in the American Revolution, and in 1787, Delaware was the first state to approve of, or *ratify*, the United States Constitution.

Making chemicals is a big industry in the state. The chemical industry is centered in the northern part of the state, north of the Chesapeake and Delaware Canal. More Delawareans work in the chemical industry than in any other line of work. South of the canal, the main activity is farming. Chickens, corn, and soybeans are important products.

Among other sights, visitors to Delaware can sample the state's long history. Swedes and Finns landed in Delaware in 1638, and some of the buildings they built are still standing in Wilmington.

Delaware is the second smallest state in area, after Rhode Island. Most of Delaware is a low plain, but there are some hills in the north. Winters are cool, and summers are hot.

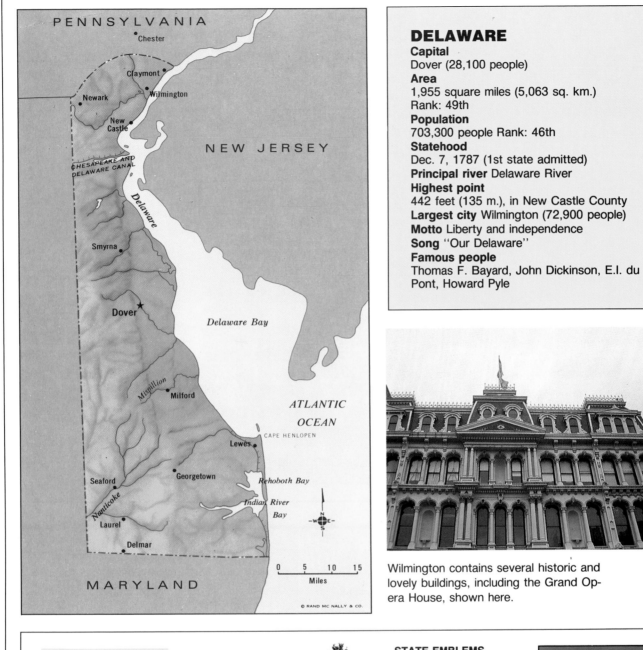

DELAWARE

Capital
Dover (28,100 people)
Area
1,955 square miles (5,063 sq. km.)
Rank: 49th
Population
703,300 people Rank: 46th
Statehood
Dec. 7, 1787 (1st state admitted)
Principal river Delaware River
Highest point
442 feet (135 m.), in New Castle County
Largest city Wilmington (72,900 people)
Motto Liberty and independence
Song "Our Delaware"
Famous people
Thomas F. Bayard, John Dickinson, E.I. du Pont, Howard Pyle

Wilmington contains several historic and lovely buildings, including the Grand Opera House, shown here.

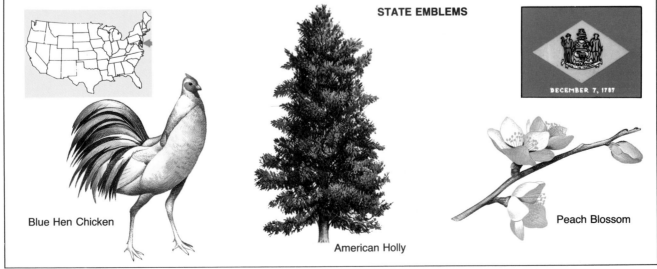

STATE EMBLEMS

Blue Hen Chicken

American Holly

Peach Blossom

Florida

Cape Canaveral, on Florida's east coast, is home of the huge Kennedy Space Center. Since 1947, Cape Canaveral has been the chief launching site for United States space exploration. Space shuttles, like the one shown here, can be reused for new missions.

The Everglades is a huge Florida marsh dotted with small, low islands called *hammocks*. Unusual plants and wild animals thrive in the portion of the swamp set aside as Everglades National Park. Wildlife here includes alligators, cougars, herons, and bald eagles.

Tourism is big business in Florida. In winter, Florida's warm climate draws many northerners seeking vacations away from the cold. Additionally, many special attractions, such as Walt Disney World, bring millions of tourists to Florida every year. Many Floridians have jobs that are related to the tourism industry—at a resort or theme park, for example. Because many people relocate to Florida after they retire, the state has a large population over the age of sixty-five.

It is said that Juan Ponce de León was searching for the Fountain of Youth when he discovered Florida in 1513. In 1565, the Spanish founded St. Augustine, the first permanent settlement in the continental United States.

Florida has more coastline than any other state except Alaska, and it is farther south than any other state except Hawaii. The land is mostly flat and low. Florida's hot summers and mild winters are good for growing some crops, especially citrus fruits such as oranges and grapefruits.

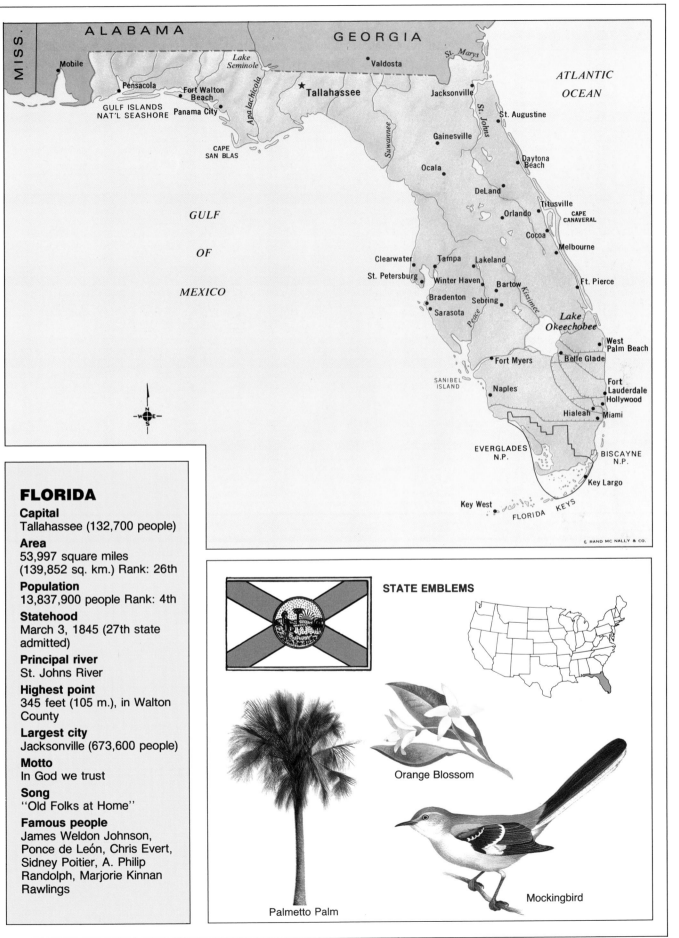

FLORIDA

Capital
Tallahassee (132,700 people)

Area
53,997 square miles
(139,852 sq. km.) Rank: 26th

Population
13,837,900 people Rank: 4th

Statehood
March 3, 1845 (27th state
admitted)

Principal river
St. Johns River

Highest point
345 feet (105 m.), in Walton
County

Largest city
Jacksonville (673,600 people)

Motto
In God we trust

Song
''Old Folks at Home''

Famous people
James Weldon Johnson,
Ponce de León, Chris Evert,
Sidney Poitier, A. Philip
Randolph, Marjorie Kinnan
Rawlings

STATE EMBLEMS

Orange Blossom

Palmetto Palm

Mockingbird

Georgia

Visitors travel by boat to Cumberland Island National Seashore. The island was once inhabited but is now a wilderness area. Among other attractions, visitors can enjoy the island's quiet beauty, abundant wildlife, and Civil War–era historic sites.

Cotton was once king in Georgia. Like many other people the South, Georgians began growing large crops of cotton after the revolutionary war. Soon the state's economy began to depend on cotton and on the plantations on which the cotton was grown. These plantations were based on slave labor. After the Civil War brought an end to slavery, many of the plantations could not survive. Cotton is still grown in Georgia, but today, other types of farming are more important.

Although Europeans first came to the region much earlier, Georgia's first city was Savannah, settled in 1733. In 1838, disputes with American Indians ended when the government forced all Cherokee people in the area to lands in the West. Georgia suffered much physical and economic damage in the Civil War.

Georgia's terrain varies from mountains in the northwest to coastal plain in the east. The climate is humid, with hot summers and mild winters.

Atlanta was a large city by the time of the Civil War, and it served as a center for the Confederacy. The North captured Atlanta in 1864 and burned most of its buildings. Atlanta made a comeback, and today it is the biggest and busiest city in the Southeast.

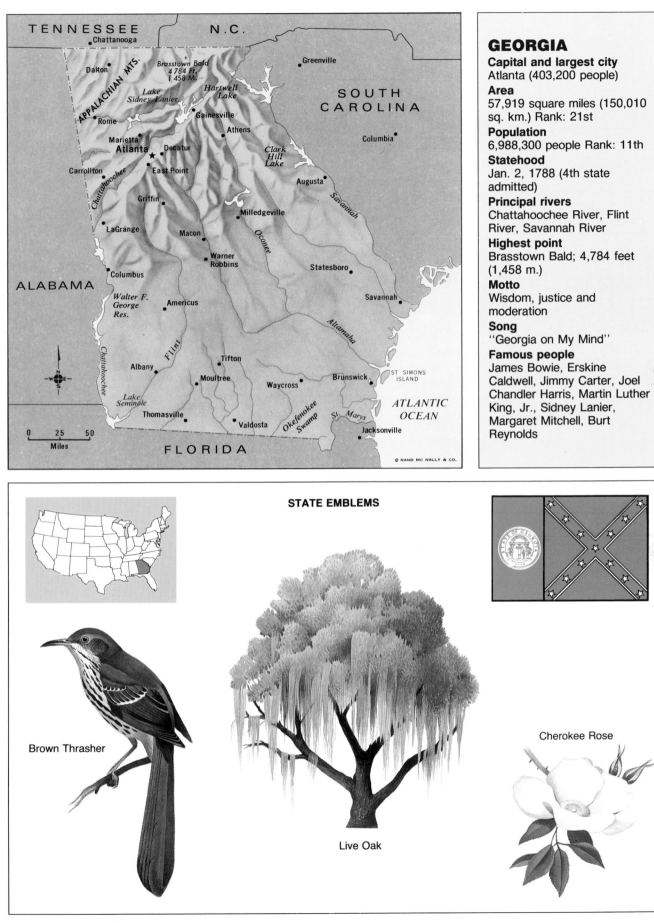

GEORGIA

Capital and largest city
Atlanta (403,200 people)

Area
57,919 square miles (150,010 sq. km.) Rank: 21st

Population
6,988,300 people Rank: 11th

Statehood
Jan. 2, 1788 (4th state admitted)

Principal rivers
Chattahoochee River, Flint River, Savannah River

Highest point
Brasstown Bald; 4,784 feet (1,458 m.)

Motto
Wisdom, justice and moderation

Song
"Georgia on My Mind"

Famous people
James Bowie, Erskine Caldwell, Jimmy Carter, Joel Chandler Harris, Martin Luther King, Jr., Sidney Lanier, Margaret Mitchell, Burt Reynolds

STATE EMBLEMS

Brown Thrasher

Live Oak

Cherokee Rose

Hawaii

Hawaii is more than America's tropical paradise. The islands have long been a stopping place for travelers crossing the huge Pacific Ocean, and they have also been a melting pot for Eastern, Western, and Pacific cultures. Today, Hawaii's location in the South Pacific makes it an important military base for the United States.

Polynesians settled the Hawaiian Islands long before the arrival of Captain James Cook of Britain in 1778. After a Japanese attack on Pearl Harbor, Oahu, on December 7, 1941, the United States entered World War II. Hawaii became the fiftieth state in 1959.

Hawaii is composed of about 130 islands, but there are eight main islands. Although the island of Hawaii is the largest island, about 80 percent of all Hawaiians live on the island of Oahu.

Vacationers from all over the world are drawn to Hawaii's year-round mild climate, sandy beaches, and spectacular volcanic scenery. Temperatures in Hawaii do not vary greatly between seasons or between day and night.

Honolulu's Waikiki Beach, on the island of Oahu, is one of the most popular tourist destinations in the world. Oahu is also home to Pearl Harbor, one of the country's naval bases. In the distance is Diamond Head, an extinct volcano.

Hawaiians invented surfing and were already holding surfing contests when Europeans first came to Hawaii in the 1700s. Huge waves of the vast Pacific Ocean roll in at great heights on several Hawaiian coasts and make the islands one of the world's best places to surf.

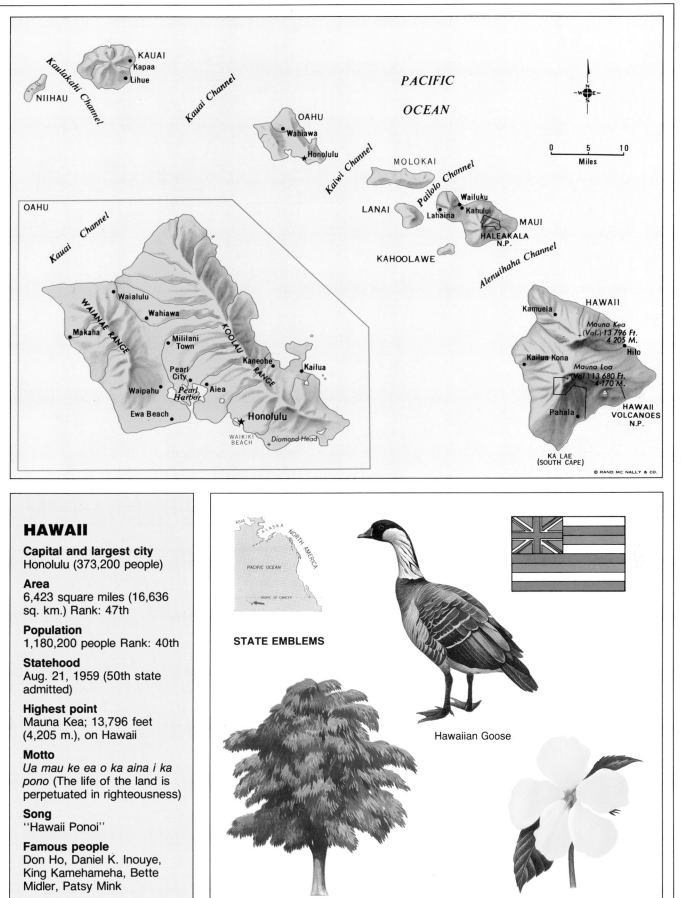

KAUAI
Kapaa
Lihue
Kaulakahi Channel
NIIHAU
Kauai Channel

OAHU
Wahiawa
Honolulu

PACIFIC OCEAN

Kaiwi Channel

MOLOKAI

Pailolo Channel

LANAI

Wailuku
Kahului
Lahaina
MAUI
HALEAKALA N.P.

KAHOOLAWE

Alenuihaha Channel

Miles
0   5   10

OAHU
Kauai Channel

WAIANAE RANGE
Waialulu
Wahiawa
Makaha
Mililani Town
KOOLAU RANGE
Pearl City
Kaneohe
Kailua
Waipahu
Pearl Harbor
Aiea
Ewa Beach
Honolulu
WAIKIKI BEACH
Diamond Head

HAWAII
Kamuela
Mauna Kea (Vol.) 13,796 Ft. 4,205 M.
Kailua Kona
Hilo
Mauna Loa (Vol.) 13,680 Ft. 4,170 M.
Pahala
HAWAII VOLCANOES N.P.
KA LAE (SOUTH CAPE)

© RAND MC NALLY & CO.

HAWAII

Capital and largest city
Honolulu (373,200 people)

Area
6,423 square miles (16,636 sq. km.) Rank: 47th

Population
1,180,200 people Rank: 40th

Statehood
Aug. 21, 1959 (50th state admitted)

Highest point
Mauna Kea; 13,796 feet (4,205 m.), on Hawaii

Motto
Ua mau ke ea o ka aina i ka pono (The life of the land is perpetuated in righteousness)

Song
"Hawaii Ponoi"

Famous people
Don Ho, Daniel K. Inouye, King Kamehameha, Bette Midler, Patsy Mink

STATE EMBLEMS

ASIA
ALASKA
NORTH AMERICA
PACIFIC OCEAN
TROPIC OF CANCER

Hawaiian Goose

Candlenut

Hibiscus

Idaho

Some travelers to Idaho come to the Snake River, which has been important to the state's history and economy. Pictured here is Hells Canyon, which is along the Idaho–Oregon border and is the deepest gorge in North America. In some areas, the canyon's walls can be a mile high.

In the 1800s, gold and silver rushes in the West brought people who very quickly created towns. As the promise of riches subsided, people sometimes abandoned the area, leaving ghost towns. Silver City, Idaho, is a ghost town that is today a tourist attraction.

Farming is the most important activity in Idaho, and potatoes are the most important crop. Idahoans also grow wheat and hay, and they raise cattle and sheep. Farming and settlement are centered on the Snake River Plain, where the land is easily tilled and where water for irrigating crops is available.

Idaho is a popular spot for skiing in the winter. People also come to the state to enjoy other outdoor sports and to view Idaho's beautiful scenery.

The Lewis and Clark Expedition passed through Idaho in 1805 and 1806. Gold was discovered in Idaho in 1860. More and more people came and wanted to live on Indian lands, and battles broke out between the settlers and the Indians.

The Rocky Mountains dominate much of Idaho's terrain. Only the strip of land called the Snake River Plain is level. Idaho has cold winters and fairly cool summers. In winter, there is heavy snowfall in the mountains.

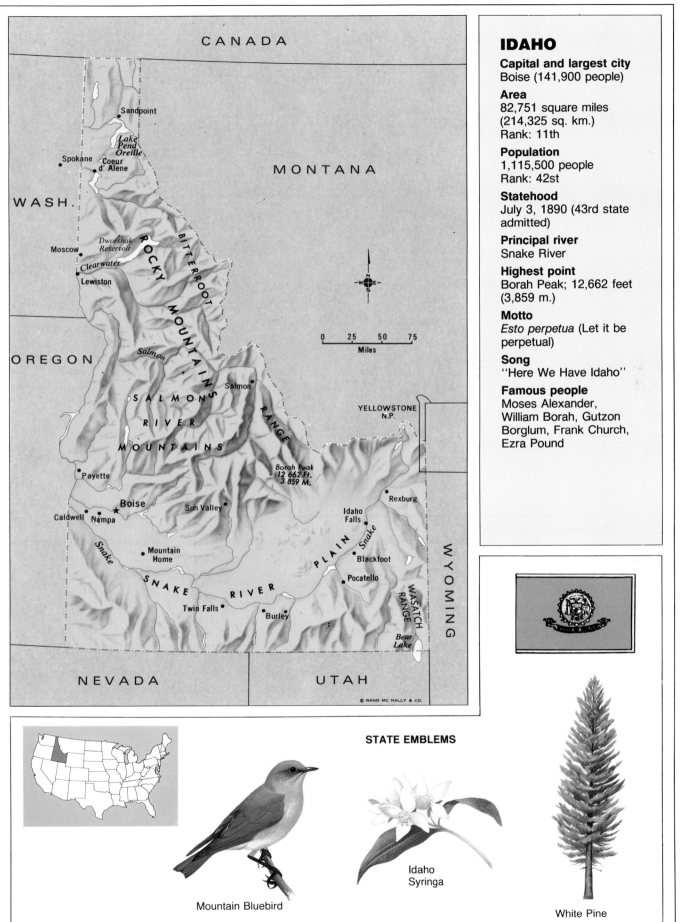

IDAHO

Capital and largest city
Boise (141,900 people)

Area
82,751 square miles
(214,325 sq. km.)
Rank: 11th

Population
1,115,500 people
Rank: 42st

Statehood
July 3, 1890 (43rd state
admitted)

Principal river
Snake River

Highest point
Borah Peak; 12,662 feet
(3,859 m.)

Motto
Esto perpetua (Let it be
perpetual)

Song
"Here We Have Idaho"

Famous people
Moses Alexander,
William Borah, Gutzon
Borglum, Frank Church,
Ezra Pound

STATE EMBLEMS

Mountain Bluebird

Idaho
Syringa

White Pine

Illinois

Shown here is a farm near the northwestern town of Galena. The farms of Illinois produce a variety of crops, with corn and soybeans the most important. Illinois farmers also raise hogs, beef cattle, and sheep.

The character of Illinois has two sides. One is urban and industrial, and it is found mostly in the northern part of the state, especially in and around Chicago. The other side is rural and agricultural, and it is found mostly in the south. Illinoisans make heavy machinery and other products, and they grow corn and soybeans.

Although French explorers and traders began to crisscross the northern Midwest in the late 1600s, the area remained largely unpopulated until the 1800s. By the mid 1800s, several Illinois cities—including Chicago—had grown up. Illinois quickly grew into one of the wealthiest and most populous states, and it remains so today.

Most of Illinois is flat, with hilly areas in the northwest and south. Illinois has cold winters and hot summers.

One reason tourists come to Illinois is to visit Chicago. Chicago is the third largest city in the United States, after New York City and Los Angeles, and it has many sports teams and cultural and historic sights.

The early days of Abraham Lincoln's political career were spent in and around Springfield. Before he was elected president, he served in the Illinois legislature and practiced law in Springfield. Lincoln is buried just outside the city, at Lincoln Tomb State Historic Site.

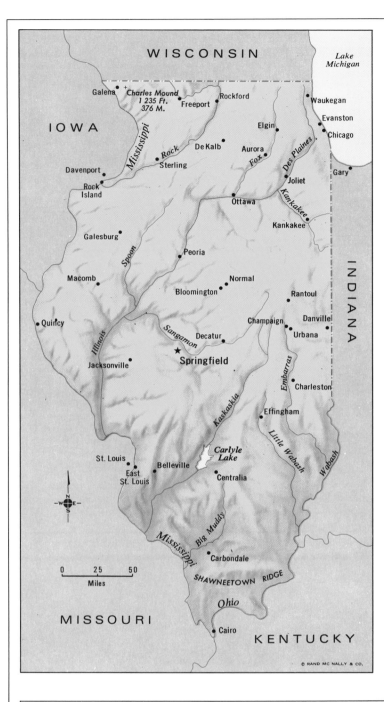

ILLINOIS

Capital
Springfield (107,500 people)

Area
55,593 square miles (143,986 sq. km.)
Rank: 24th

Population
11,737,600 people Rank: 6th

Statehood
Dec. 3, 1818 (21st state admitted)

Principal rivers
Illinois River, Mississippi River, Ohio River

Highest point
Charles Mound; 1,235 feet (376 m.)

Largest city
Chicago (2,762,000 people)

Motto
State sovereignty-national union

Song
"Illinois"

Famous people
Jane Addams, Walt Disney, Ulysses S. Grant, Jesse Jackson, Abraham Lincoln, Carl Sandburg

Historic Galena was once Illinois's leading city. Today, Chicago is.

STATE EMBLEMS

Illinois
Native Violet

White Oak

Cardinal

Indiana

Indiana Dunes National Lakeshore, home to a variety of plants and animals, is a wilderness area along Lake Michigan. The dunes are especially important to Indiana's wildlife because the area around them is urban, with factories, houses, and other buildings.

Every Memorial Day weekend, the Indianapolis 500 Auto Race takes place just west of downtown Indianapolis. The 500-mile (805-kilometer) race is one of the most prestigious automobile races in the world and is preceded by a month-long celebration.

No one knows what happened to the Mound Builders, an ancient people who lived in what is now Indiana. They disappeared long before Europeans arrived, leaving behind many artifacts and ruins.

When the French came in 1679, many other Indian groups inhabited Indiana. Later on, pioneers battled with the Indians, who suffered a major loss at Tippecanoe in 1811. Settlement increased after the first railroads across the state were constructed in the mid 1800s.

Indianans who work in factories make metals, machinery, and motor vehicles. Other people are farmers who grow corn, soybeans, and wheat.

Indiana's terrain includes northern lakes, central plains, and southern hills. From the air, the landscape looks like a colorful patchwork quilt, because Indiana was divided into squares in the 1700s to ensure orderly settlement. Like much of the Midwest, Indiana has very hot, humid summers, and very cold, snowy winters.

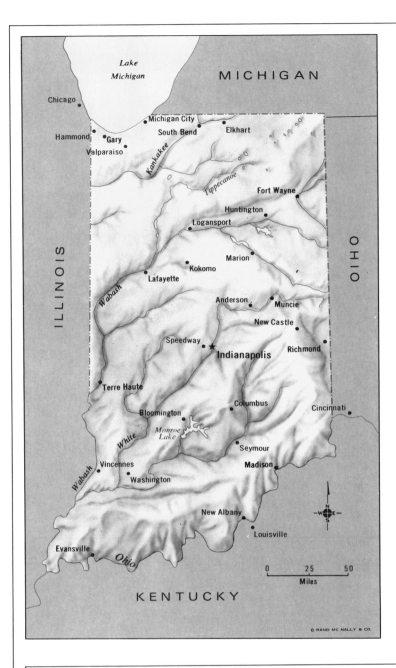

INDIANA

Capital and largest city
Indianapolis (760,700 people)

Area
35,870 square miles (92,903 sq. km.)
Rank: 38th

Population
5,740,700 people Rank: 14th

Statehood
Dec. 11, 1816 (19th state admitted)

Principal rivers
Ohio River, Wabash River

Highest point
1,257 feet (383 m.), in Wayne County

Motto
Crossroads of America

Song
"On the Banks of the Wabash, Far Away"

Famous people
Hoagy Carmichael, Theodore Dreiser, Michael Jackson, Cole Porter, Ernie Pyle, Booth Tarkington

This covered bridge is one of the sights of rural Indiana.

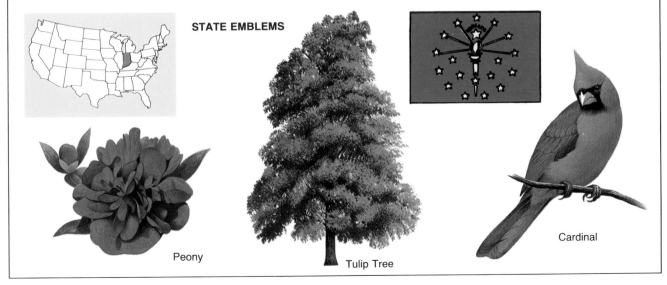

STATE EMBLEMS

Peony

Tulip Tree

Cardinal

Iowa

Thousands of years ago, glaciers covered much of what is now Iowa. When they melted, the glaciers left rich, fertile soils and gently rolling hills, which are well suited for farming.

Today, many Iowans are somehow involved with farming. Many people grow crops—mainly corn and soybeans—and raise livestock; other people work at turning those items into food products. Farm machinery is also made.

Like other states in the Midwest, Iowa is far from an ocean or other large body of water and the modifying effects water has on climate. Iowans therefore experience hot summers and cold winters.

It is believed that Iowa was inhabited by the Mound Builders as much as thirteen thousand years ago, but the first Europeans to come to the area were the French in the late 1600s. Iowa was included in the Louisiana Purchase in 1803. Thousands of settlers arrived after statehood was granted in 1846, many of them European immigrants seeking land to farm.

Iowa's small towns reinforce the state's reputation as the typical midwestern state. Shown here is Eldorado, a town of about one hundred people in the northeast. Despite Iowa's reputation as a rural state, more Iowans live in urban areas than in rural areas.

The plains of the Midwest form one of the world's most productive agricultural regions. Farmers today are aided by machines, but agriculture here began with horses and plows. The history of farming in Iowa and the Midwest is recreated at the Living History Farms near Des Moines.

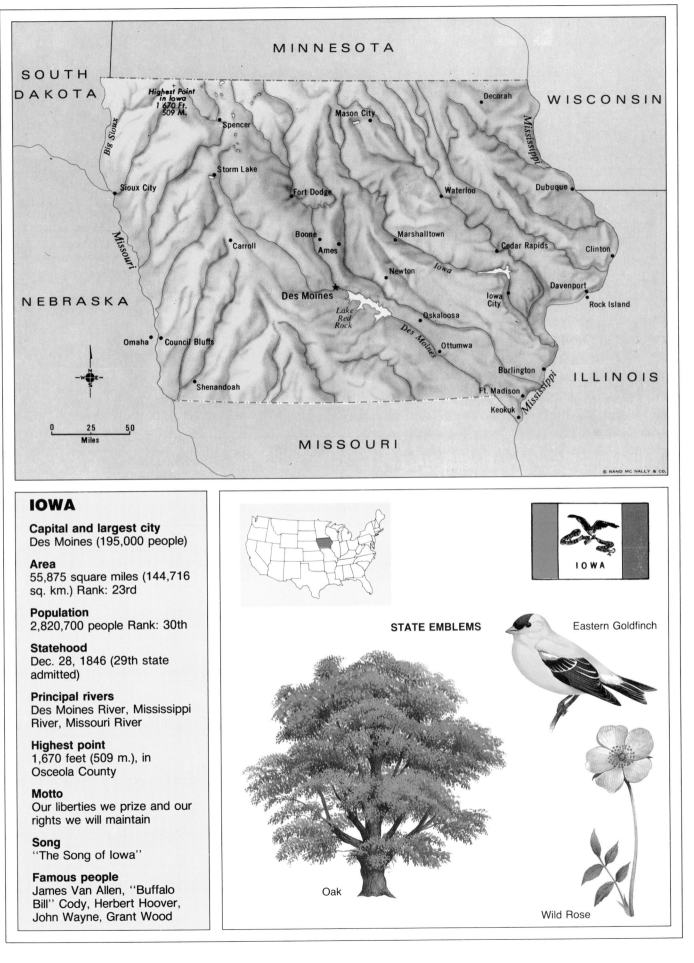

MINNESOTA

SOUTH DAKOTA

WISCONSIN

+ Highest Point in Iowa 1,670 Ft. 509 M.

Big Sioux

Decorah

Mason City

Spencer

Mississippi

Storm Lake

Sioux City

Fort Dodge

Waterloo

Dubuque

Missouri

Boone

Marshalltown

Ames

Cedar Rapids

Clinton

NEBRASKA

Carroll

Newton

Iowa

Davenport

Des Moines

Lake Red Rock

Iowa City

Rock Island

Oskaloosa

Omaha • Council Bluffs

Des Moines

Ottumwa

ILLINOIS

Shenandoah

Burlington

Mississippi

Ft. Madison

Keokuk

N W E S

0 25 50
Miles

MISSOURI

© RAND MC NALLY & CO.

IOWA

Capital and largest city
Des Moines (195,000 people)

Area
55,875 square miles (144,716 sq. km.) Rank: 23rd

Population
2,820,700 people Rank: 30th

Statehood
Dec. 28, 1846 (29th state admitted)

Principal rivers
Des Moines River, Mississippi River, Missouri River

Highest point
1,670 feet (509 m.), in Osceola County

Motto
Our liberties we prize and our rights we will maintain

Song
"The Song of Iowa"

Famous people
James Van Allen, "Buffalo Bill" Cody, Herbert Hoover, John Wayne, Grant Wood

IOWA

STATE EMBLEMS

Eastern Goldfinch

Oak

Wild Rose

Kansas

Author Laura Ingalls Wilder wrote a classic series of children's tales about life on the United States frontier. A reproduction of a log cabin that Wilder and her family lived in has been built on the prairie southwest of Independence.

Wheat fields are common in Kansas, which is one of the greatest grain-producing regions in the world. Modern farming machines do much of the work, so fewer people can farm more land. This means that as the farms are growing bigger, the farm population is getting smaller.

To the Plains Indians, Kansas offered huge herds of bison, which the Indians hunted. To early European settlers, however, the Great Plains of Kansas represented a desert that was unfit for habitation.

As a result, settlers merely passed through Kansas in the early days of the United States on their way to more desirable lands farther west. Later on, the United States government sent Indians from other places to reservations set up in Kansas because it was thought that the land could not be used.

In the 1860s and 1870s, after the first railroads were built across the United States, more people began to settle in Kansas. Then, immigrants brought a new kind of wheat that required very little moisture to the Great Plains, and the story of Kansas changed. The wheat thrived, and Kansas became a land of prosperous farms. It remains so today, with wheat the major crop of western Kansas, and corn most important in the east. Kansans experience hot summers and cold winters.

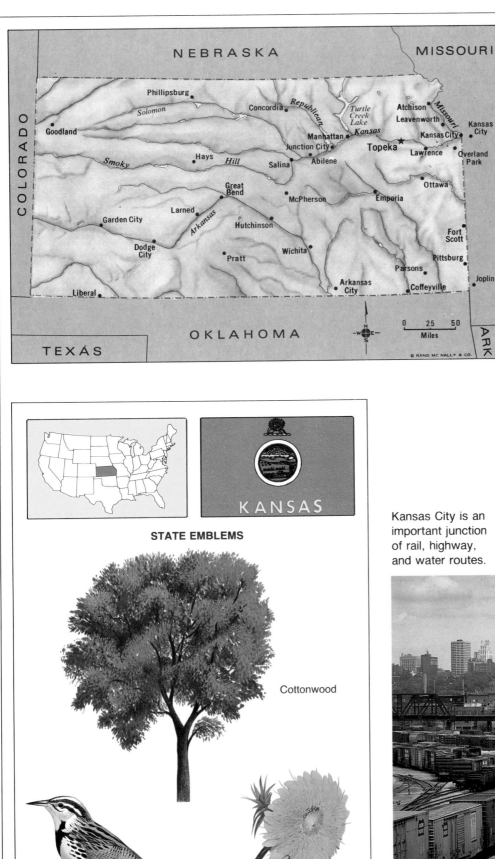

KANSAS

Capital
Topeka (121,000 people)

Area
81,823 square miles
(211,922 sq. km.)
Rank: 13th

Population
2,548,300 people
Rank: 32nd

Statehood
Jan. 29, 1861 (34th
state admitted)

Principal rivers
Arkansas River, Kansas
River

Highest point
Mount Sunflower; 4,039
feet (1,231 m.)

Largest city
Wichita (315,100 people)

Motto
Ad astra per aspera (To
the stars through
difficulties)

Song
"Home on the Range"

Famous people
Thomas Hart Benton,
Amelia Earhart, Dwight
D. Eisenhower, Carry
Nation, William Allen
White

STATE EMBLEMS

Cottonwood

Western Meadowlark

Sunflower

Kansas City is an
important junction
of rail, highway,
and water routes.

Kentucky

In the Bluegrass region surrounding Lexington lies Kentucky's best farmlands, grazing land, and tobacco fields. Many of the nation's finest horses come from the Bluegrass region, which is named after a silver-blue grass that grows here.

Travelers might come to Kentucky to see the Kentucky Derby, a Thoroughbred horse race run at Churchill Downs racetrack in Louisville. Held every May for more than one hundred years, the Derby is the most famous and important horse race in the United States. Visitors to the state can also enjoy Kentucky's federal and state parks and historic sites.

Ancestors of American Indians were living in Kentucky more than thirteen thousand years ago. Only a few Europeans entered Kentucky before 1750 because the Appalachian Mountains slowed exploration and settlement of the region. Kentucky was on the border between the North and South in the Civil War, and Kentuckians were found in both armies.

Kentucky's factories produce metals and machinery, while on its farms, tobacco is grown and livestock is raised.

Kentucky's terrain features rolling hills, broad valleys, and rugged mountains. Summers are hot, and winters are short and have little snow.

Mammoth Cave National Park, near Bowling Green, is a huge maze of underground passages. It was formed over thousands of years by acidic water trickling though limestone. The cave has never been fully explored and may be the largest cave system in the world.

KENTUCKY

Capital
Frankfort (28,100 people)

Area
39,732 square miles (102,906 sq. km.) Rank: 36th

Population
3,798,100 people Rank: 24th

Statehood
June 1, 1792 (15th state admitted)

Principal rivers
Cumberland River, Kentucky River, Ohio River

Highest point
Black Mountain; 4,139 feet (1,262 m.)

Largest city
Louisville (271,800 people)

Motto
United we stand, divided we fall

Song
"My Old Kentucky Home"

Famous people
Muhammad Ali, John James Audubon, Daniel Boone, Loretta Lynn, Whitney M. Young

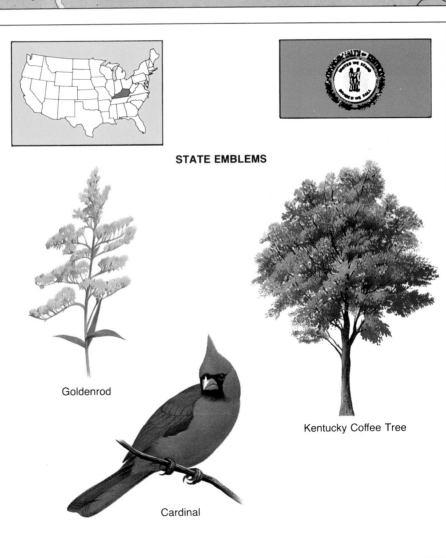

STATE EMBLEMS

Goldenrod

Kentucky Coffee Tree

Cardinal

Louisiana

In the late 1700s, many French Canadians left their home-land and settled in the marshes, or *bayous*, of Louisiana. The descendants of these people, known as Cajuns, still live in the region and retain their own language, cuisine, and customs.

New Orleans was founded by the French in 1718. Until it became part of the United States in 1803, it changed hands between the French and Spanish. This heritage can been seen in the Spanish-style architecture of the historic French Quarter, shown here.

Mardi Gras, French for "fat Tuesday," is an annual celebration in which people enjoy themselves on the last day before Lent, traditionally a period of fasting. Mardi Gras celebrations are held in several places around the world; one of the most famous takes place in New Orleans. Thousands of people come to New Orleans every year to watch the torchlight parades, street dancing, costume balls, and masquerades.

In 1803, the United States bought the land between the Mississippi River and the Rocky Mountains from France. This transaction is known as the Louisiana Purchase. Louisiana was the first state to enter the United States from this region.

Mining for oil and natural gas is important in Louisiana. The state produces more oil than any other except Alaska and Texas, and Louisiana is the country's leader in producing natural gas.

The land consists mainly of flat coastal plain. Louisianians experience long, hot summers and short, mild winters.

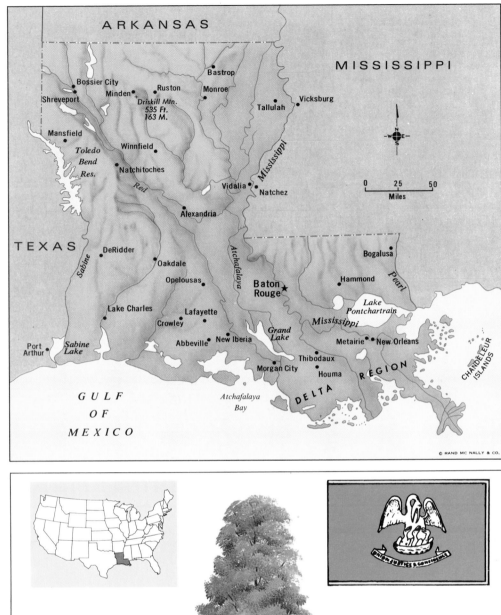

LOUISIANA

Capital
Baton Rouge (225,900 people)

Area
43,566 square miles (112,836 sq. km.)
Rank: 33rd

Population
4,308,300 people
Rank: 21st

Statehood
April 30, 1812 (18th state admitted)

Principal rivers
Mississippi River, Red River, Sabine River

Highest point
Driskill Mountain; 535 feet (163 m.)

Largest city
New Orleans (494,800 people)

Motto
Union, justice, and confidence

Song
"Give Me Louisiana"

Famous people
Louis Armstrong, Pierre Beauregard, Lillian Hellman, Mahalia Jackson, Huey Long

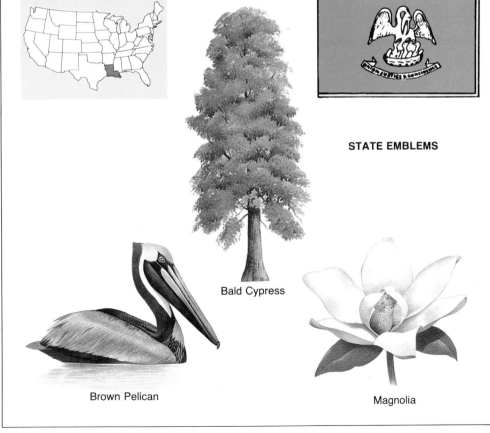

STATE EMBLEMS

Bald Cypress

Brown Pelican

Magnolia

Maine

The farthest point east in the United States is Eastport, Maine. Locals insist that the morning sun strikes first in Eastport, and the area is nicknamed Sunrise County.

The first Europeans to reach North America might have been the Vikings, who probably ventured to Maine from Greenland or Iceland in about A.D. 1000. Maine figured prominently in some of the first wars fought on American soil: the French and Indian Wars, the American Revolution, and the War of 1812.

Many Mainers have jobs in the leather-goods industry, making shoes and other footwear. Articles made from wood are also produced, and farmers raise livestock and potatoes.

Some of Maine's coast is low, but much of the state in hilly or mountainous. The Appalachian Mountains—the major mountain range of the eastern United States—extend into Maine. Residents of Maine experience long, cold winters and short, cool summers. In summer, Maine's refreshingly cool weather and beautiful scenery draw many vacationers from the hot cities of the Northeast.

Maine's rocky coastline, represented here by Acadia National Park, was formed by glaciers. Acadia, New England's only national park, contains mountains, lakes, and seashore. It includes a small area on the mainland and much of Mount Desert Island and Isle au Haut.

Lobsters are saltwater crustaceans that are a popular delicacy. The largest of all lobsters might be the American lobster, which thrives along the Atlantic coast, especially in the cool waters off Maine. Maine's annual lobster catch is the largest of any state.

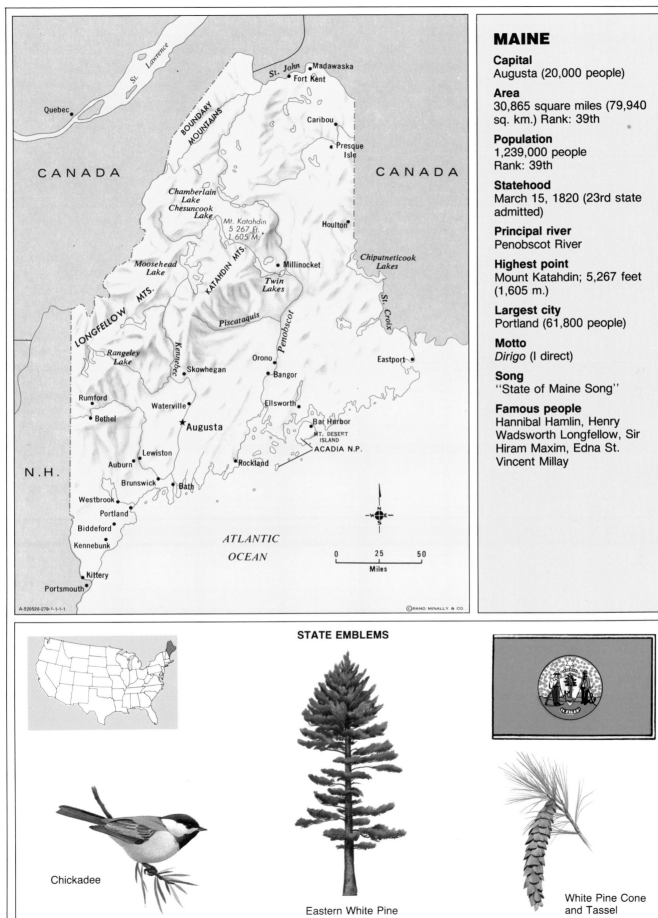

MAINE

Capital
Augusta (20,000 people)

Area
30,865 square miles (79,940 sq. km.) Rank: 39th

Population
1,239,000 people
Rank: 39th

Statehood
March 15, 1820 (23rd state admitted)

Principal river
Penobscot River

Highest point
Mount Katahdin; 5,267 feet (1,605 m.)

Largest city
Portland (61,800 people)

Motto
Dirigo (I direct)

Song
"State of Maine Song"

Famous people
Hannibal Hamlin, Henry Wadsworth Longfellow, Sir Hiram Maxim, Edna St. Vincent Millay

A-520520-279-1-1-1-1

©RAND McNALLY & CO.

STATE EMBLEMS

Chickadee

Eastern White Pine

White Pine Cone and Tassel

Maryland

Settled in the 1600s, Annapolis played an important role in the early days of the United States. Since 1845, it has been the site of the United States Naval Academy. Today, the city on Chesapeake Bay boasts more than eighty buildings erected before the revolutionary war.

Maryland shares Assateague Island National Seashore with Virginia. Among Assateague's many wild animals is the Chincoteague pony, descended from the horses of early explorers. These ponies are the subject of Marguerite Henry's *Misty of Chincoteague* and other titles.

Much United States history has taken place in Maryland. Among the historic sites is Fort McHenry, where the battle that inspired Francis Scott Key to write "The Star-Spangled Banner" took place. The song is now the national anthem of the United States.

Maryland was divided between North—the Union states—and South—the Confederate States—in the Civil War. But Abraham Lincoln, who was president at the time, forced Maryland to stay in the Union because Washington, D.C., the Union's capi-tal, was situated in Maryland.

Many Marylanders work in factories, making steel and assembling cars, tools, and other products made from metal. Fishing is also important, as Chesapeake Bay yields large amounts of oysters, crabs, fish, and clams.

Chesapeake Bay's waters occupy a great part of eastern Maryland. The flat land near the bay gradually rises into the Blue Ridge and the Appalachians of the west. In the east, summers are hot and winters, cool; temperatures are lower in the higher elevations of the west.

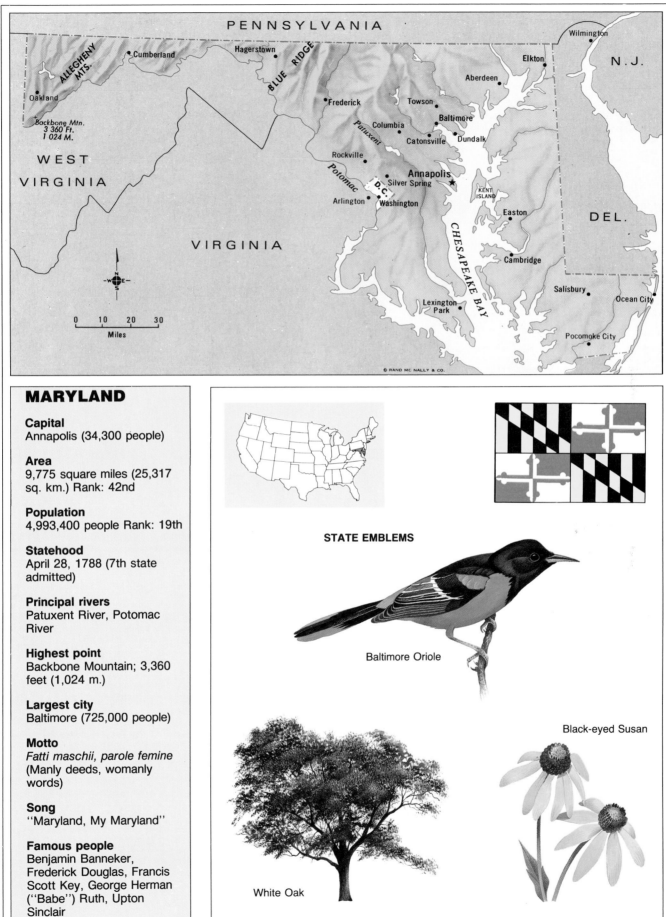

MARYLAND

Capital
Annapolis (34,300 people)

Area
9,775 square miles (25,317 sq. km.) Rank: 42nd

Population
4,993,400 people Rank: 19th

Statehood
April 28, 1788 (7th state admitted)

Principal rivers
Patuxent River, Potomac River

Highest point
Backbone Mountain; 3,360 feet (1,024 m.)

Largest city
Baltimore (725,000 people)

Motto
Fatti maschii, parole femine (Manly deeds, womanly words)

Song
"Maryland, My Maryland"

Famous people
Benjamin Banneker, Frederick Douglas, Francis Scott Key, George Herman ("Babe") Ruth, Upton Sinclair

STATE EMBLEMS

Baltimore Oriole

Black-eyed Susan

White Oak

Massachusetts

The "hook" of Massachusetts is a sandy peninsula called Cape Cod. The Cape is about 70 miles (125 kilometers) long and has many sights to see, including Cape Cod National Seashore, shown here. Historic towns, such as Provincetown, are known for their quaint charm.

U nited States history began when Paul Revere set out from his house on the famous midnight ride that marked the beginning of the American Revolution. Massachusetts has one of the longest histories of any of the states, and it boasts many historic sites, including Paul Revere's house, still standing in Boston.

In the early days of the Industrial Revolution in the United States, Massachusetts became a manufacturing leader. It remains so today, with electronic and electrical equipment and other types of machinery the most important products. Fishing is another traditional occupation, and the waters around Massachusetts today yield, among other kinds of seafood, large catches of sea scallops.

The land of Massachusetts contains coastal plains and part of the Appalachian range. The islands of Nantucket and Martha's Vineyard belong to Massachusetts. Although ocean breezes help cool the coast, summers are warm, while winters are long and cold.

The *Mayflower* landed at Plymouth Rock, Massachusetts, on December 21, 1620. Its 102 passengers were known as Pilgrims, and they founded one of the earliest permanent English settlements in the New World. American Indians helped the Pilgrims survive.

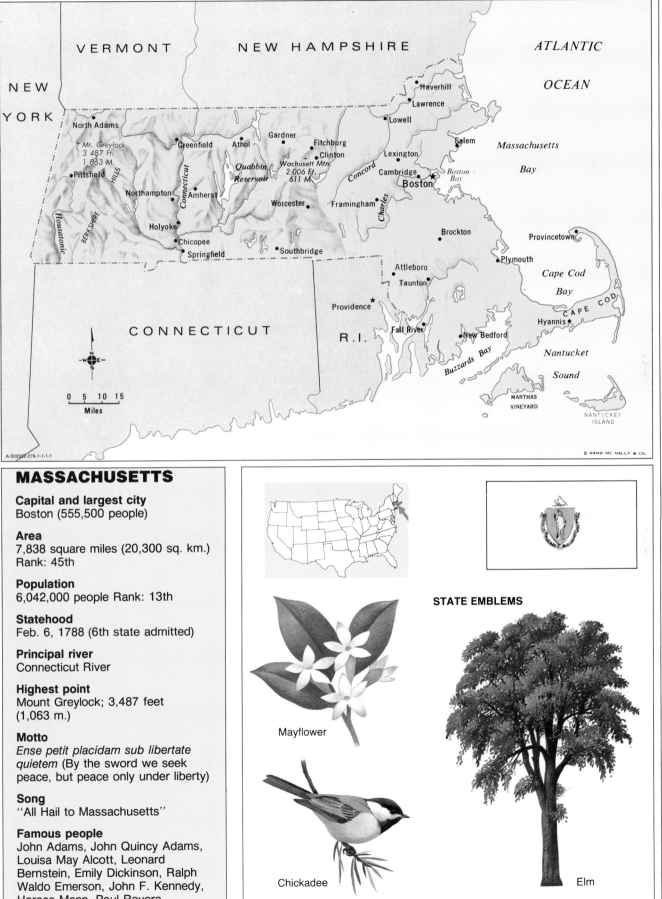

MASSACHUSETTS

Capital and largest city
Boston (555,500 people)

Area
7,838 square miles (20,300 sq. km.)
Rank: 45th

Population
6,042,000 people Rank: 13th

Statehood
Feb. 6, 1788 (6th state admitted)

Principal river
Connecticut River

Highest point
Mount Greylock; 3,487 feet
(1,063 m.)

Motto
Ense petit placidam sub libertate quietem (By the sword we seek peace, but peace only under liberty)

Song
"All Hail to Massachusetts"

Famous people
John Adams, John Quincy Adams, Louisa May Alcott, Leonard Bernstein, Emily Dickinson, Ralph Waldo Emerson, John F. Kennedy, Horace Mann, Paul Revere

STATE EMBLEMS

Mayflower

Chickadee

Elm

Michigan

Isle Royale National Park is made up of islands in Lake Superior. This wilderness area is the home of many wild animals, including moose and wolves. Scientists have conducted research here, studying the relationship between the hunter—the wolf—and the hunted—the moose.

On the Great Lakes–St. Lawrence Seaway system, Detroit is one of the nation's busiest ports. Ships deliver raw materials for use in the city's factories and pick up automobiles and other products. Detroit has long been considered the automobile capital of the world.

In 1903, Henry Ford established an auto factory in Michigan—an event that changed forever the state's history and economy. Motor vehicles remain the most important manufactured product in Michigan, and many people are employed in the motor vehicle industry. Travelers come to see the many sites associated with the automobile industry as well as Michigan's natural offerings.

Although the motor vehicle industry dominates the economy, farming is also significant. The most important crops are fruits and vegetables, such as cherries, cucumbers, beans, and blueberries. Livestock is also raised.

Michigan is made up of two parts: the Upper Peninsula and the Lower Peninsula. Most Michiganders live in the bottom portion of the Lower Peninsula. The land of Michigan and the Great Lakes were shaped by the glaciers that covered the region about 2,500 years ago. Michigan has cold, snowy winters and mild summers.

MICHIGAN

Capital
Lansing (127,300 people)

Area
56,809 square miles (147,135 sq. km.)
Rank: 22nd

Population
9,493,200 people
Rank: 8th

Statehood
Jan. 26, 1837 (26th state admitted)

Principal river
Muskegon River

Highest point
Mount Arvon; 1,979 feet (603 m.)

Largest city
Detroit (995,700 people)

Motto
Si quaeris peninsulam amoenam circumspice (If you seek a pleasant peninsula, look about you)

Song
"Michigan, My Michigan"

Famous people
George Custer, Thomas Dewey, Edna Ferber, Henry Ford, Robert Jarvik

STATE EMBLEMS

Robin

White Pine

Apple Blossom

Minnesota

Superior National Forest, in the northeastern corner of the state, contains more than two thousand beautiful lakes and acres and acres of wooded wilderness. This region is considered by many to be the finest canoe country in the United States.

During the last ice age, thousands of years ago, much of Minnesota and other parts of the Midwest were completely buried under thick, slow-moving sheets of ice called *glaciers*. These glaciers scoured the landscape underneath and, in Minnesota, left uncovered valuable iron deposits in the north and dumped fertile soils in other parts of the state. When the glaciers melted, they left more than fifteen thousand lakes in Minnesota. The results of this glacial action have been valuable to Minnesotans, who have mined the iron, farmed the soils, and enjoyed the lake-filled landscape.

There is evidence that Vikings from Scandinavia visited what is now Minnesota in the 1300s. After the Indians who lived in Minnesota gave up parts of their lands in the 1850s, settlers flocked to the area.

Many Minnesotans live in or near Minneapolis and St. Paul, which together are known as the Twin Cities. Winters in Minnesota are long, cold, and often severe; summers are short.

The evenly spaced farms, cities, and roads in southern Minnesota show how humans have divided the landscape. After 1850, farming became the most important occupation in Minnesota, and corn and soybeans became major crops. Manufacturing is more important than agriculture today.

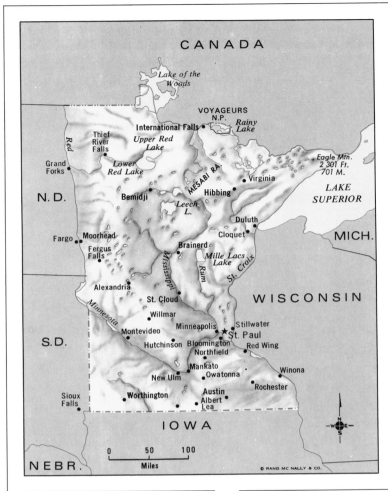

Situated near the head of the Mississippi River, Minneapolis and St. Paul are a center for business and culture in the northern Midwest.

MINNESOTA

Capital
St. Paul (268,400 people)

Area
79,617 square miles (206,208 sq. km.) Rank: 14th

Population
4,542,100 people Rank: 20th

Statehood
May 11, 1858 (32nd state admitted)

Principal rivers
Mississippi River, Red River

Highest point
Eagle Mountain; 2,301 feet (701 m.)

Largest city
Minneapolis (365,500 people)

Motto
L'Etoile du nord (The north star)

Song
"Hail! Minnesota"

Famous people
F. Scott Fitzgerald, Hubert Humphrey, Sinclair Lewis, Walter Mondale, Charles Schulz

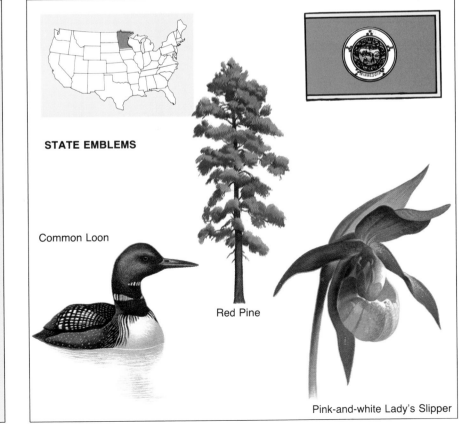

STATE EMBLEMS

Common Loon

Red Pine

Pink-and-white Lady's Slipper

Mississippi

Barrier islands lie off many coastlines in the East and South. The islands protect the mainland but are themselves subject to the forces of tides and storms, so their shapes frequently change. Many barrier islands are protected wilderness areas, such as Gulf Islands National Seashore, shown here.

In the Vicksburg Campaign of the Civil War, the North captured the town of Vicksburg. This was an important victory for the Union. It gave the North control of the Mississippi River, and it split the South's lands in two. The campaign is memorialized in a historic park.

Before the Civil War, Mississippi was a land of thriving plantations. Like its southern neighbors, Mississippi prospered by growing one principal crop: cotton. Those days are long gone, however, and now manufacturing is most important. Principal products are transportation equipment and processed foods. Some Mississippians still grow cotton, but soybeans are almost as common, and the old cotton plantations are now tourist attractions. The area around Natchez has several such plantations.

Spanish explorers came in 1540, but the first settlers were the French in 1699. The Civil War of the 1860s and the Great Depression of the 1930s both caused great economic damage in the state. In the 1960s, Mississippi was a center for the Civil Rights movement.

Mississippi consists mainly of flat plains, including part of the Mississippi River Delta, the area where the river empties into the Gulf of Mexico. Mississippi has long, hot, humid summers and short, mild winters

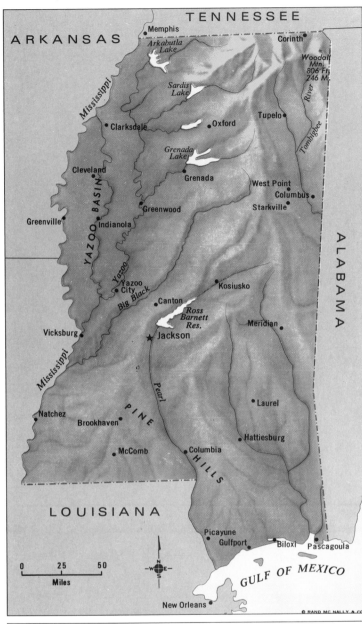

MISSISSIPPI

Capital and largest city
Jackson (196,900 people)

Area
46,914 square miles (121,507 sq. km.)
Rank: 31st

Population
2,642,700 people Rank: 31st

Statehood
Dec. 10, 1817 (20th state admitted)

Principal rivers
Mississippi River, Pearl River

Highest point
Woodall Mountain; 806 feet (246 m.)

Motto
Virtute et armis (By valor and arms)

Song
"Go, Mississippi"

Famous people
Jefferson Davis, William Faulkner, Elvis
Presley, Leontyne Price, Eudora Welty,
Tennessee Williams

Tourists can still ride steamboats up and down
the Mississippi River.

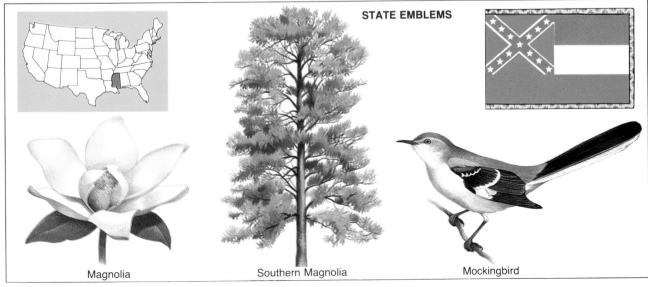

STATE EMBLEMS

Magnolia

Southern Magnolia

Mockingbird

Missouri

The Ozark National Scenic Riverways contain miles of free-flowing streams. Natural underground water reservoirs feed the area's many springs, which in turn feed the rivers. Shown here is the Alley Springs flow on the Jacks Fork River.

Mark Twain, the great American author and humorist, was raised in Hannibal, Missouri. His stories about Tom Sawyer and Huckleberry Finn recount tales of Twain's own childhood in and around Hannibal and life on the nearby Mississippi River.

Two great rivers—the Missouri and the Mississippi—meet in Missouri. The state's central location and access to waterways make it an important crossroads today, just as it was when the American West was being settled in the 1800s. St. Louis, one of the largest cities in the United States, grew up near the spot where the two rivers meet.

Transportation equipment—especially automobiles, aircraft, spacecraft, and railroad cars—is Missouri's most important manufactured product. Missourians also grow corn and soybeans and raise livestock.

Vacationers come to Missouri to enjoy the Ozarks, a series of hills and low mountains in the southern part of the state. Here are found more than four thousand caves and many large springs. Lake of the Ozarks, formed by a dam on the Osage River, is one of the world's largest humanmade lakes.

Ancient glaciers flattened northern Missouri and covered the land with rich soils. In the summer, the weather is generally hot; in winter, it is cold.

MISSOURI

Capital
Jefferson City (38,200 people)

Area
68,898 square miles (178,446 sq. km.)
Rank: 18th

Population
5,257,300 people
Rank: 16th

Statehood
Aug. 10, 1821 (24th state admitted)

Principal rivers
Mississippi River, Missouri River

Highest point
Taum Sauk Mountain; 1,772 feet (540 m.)

Largest city
Kansas City (432,500 people)

Motto
Salus populi suprema lex esto (The welfare of the people shall be the supreme law)

Song
"Missouri Waltz"

Famous people
Thomas Hart Benton, George Washington Carver, Samuel Clemens (Mark Twain), Joseph Pulitzer, Harry S Truman

STATE EMBLEMS

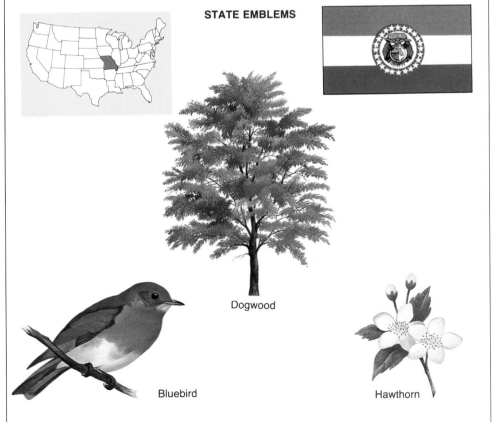

Dogwood

Bluebird

Hawthorn

The Law Courts at St. Louis framed by the Gateway to the West.

Montana

In northern Montana, Glacier National Park contains a rugged, snowcapped section of the Rocky Mountains. Many of the white areas on the peaks are *glaciers*, or huge, mobile ice masses. Melted water from the glaciers feeds the park's lakes, rivers, and waterfalls.

Eastern Montana lies in the Great Plains, a vast, nearly treeless grassland that stretches from central Texas to northern Canada and from the western Mississippi Valley to the Rocky Mountains. It is this region of wide open spaces that earned Montana the nickname Big Sky Country.

The western part of the state is dominated by the magnificent Rocky Mountains. It is this region of towering peaks that earned the name *montaña*, which is Spanish for "mountain."

In the Great Plains, summers are hot and winters are very cold. In the mountainous west, summers are cooler. In winter, warm, dry winds called *chinooks* sometimes blow into the Plains from the Rockies, bringing unexpected and dramatic rises in temperature.

A great number of Montanans are farmers. The raising of cattle and the growing of wheat are most important. Montana's forests provide lumber, and its land yields oil, copper, and coal.

For centuries, the Plains Indians and the American bison coexisted on the Great Plains. In the 1800s, settlers slaughtered millions of bison until there were only a few hundred left. Thanks to refuges such as the National Bison Range in Montana, the bison has survived.

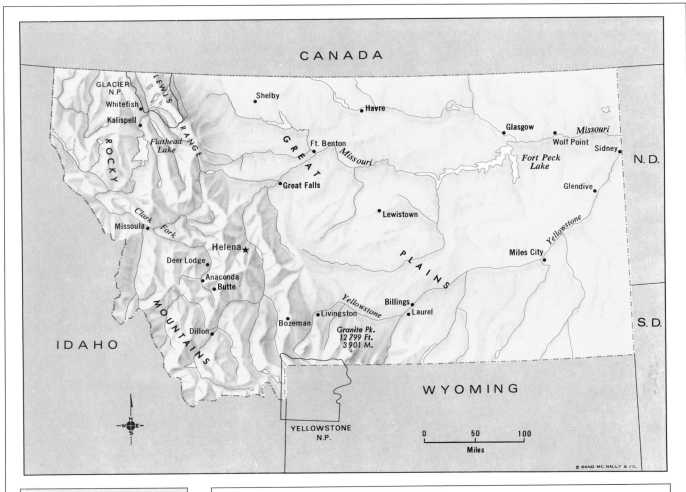

MONTANA

Capital
Helena (26,400 people)

Area
145,556 square miles
(376,990 sq. km.) Rank: 4th

Population
836,200 people Rank: 44th

Statehood
Nov. 8, 1889 (41st state
admitted)

Principal rivers
Missouri River, Yellowstone
River

Highest point
Granite Peak; 12,799 feet
(3,901 m.)

Largest city
Billings (84,200 people)

Motto
Oro y plata (Gold and silver)

Song
"Montana"

Famous people
Gary Cooper, Will James,
Mike Mansfield, Jeannette
Rankin, Charles Russell

STATE EMBLEMS

Ponderosa Pine

Bitterroot

Western Meadowlark

Nebraska

In Agate Fossil Beds National Monument are the remains of mammals that thrived in the region about twenty-two million years ago. Here visitors can see bones of extinct animals that might have been ancestors of the modern rhinoceros, horse, pig, deer, and other mammals.

The Sand Hills of north-central Nebraska are covered with grass and are good for grazing. The grass holds the soil in place and prevents the region from turning into a dust bowl. Farmers in Nebraska and other areas now use methods that prevent dust bowls from forming.

Farmers use nearly 97 percent of Nebraska's land. Most of the state lies in the Great Plains, a huge region in central North America that was once the bottom of an ancient sea. When irrigated, the normally dry land is excellent for growing corn, the most important crop.

The Great Plains are also superb for grazing, and Nebraskans raise a large number of cattle. Summers are hot and winters are cold on the Plains.

At the time of the Civil War, Nebraska was known as "Indian country," and although the United States government offered free or inexpensive land here, there were few settlers. Statehood and the advance of rail travel brought more people, but farming the land remained difficult. Droughts, grasshoppers, and blizzards often destroyed crops and cattle. In the 1930s, the Great Depression and a series of drought years brought especially hard times. Since then, improved farming methods, including irrigation, have created prosperity.

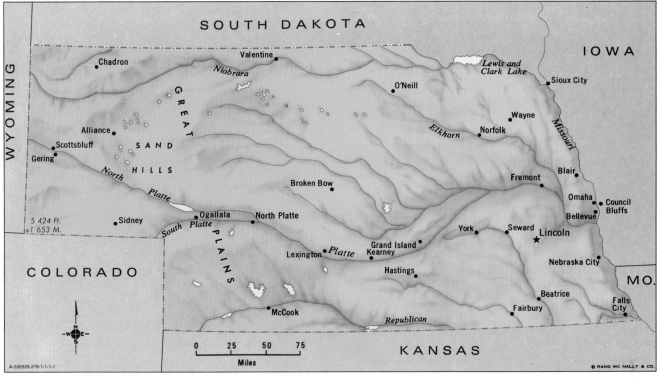

NEBRASKA

Capital
Lincoln (201,000 people)

Area
76,878 square miles (199,114 sq. km.) Rank: 15th

Population
1,612,900 people Rank: 37th

Statehood
March 1, 1867 (37th state admitted)

Principal rivers
Missouri River, Platte River

Highest point
5,424 feet (1,653 m.), in Kimball County

Largest city
Omaha (345,100 people)

Motto
Equality before the law

Song
"Beautiful Nebraska"

Famous people
Fred Astaire, Willa Cather, Johnny Carson, Henry Fonda, Gerald R. Ford, Malcolm X

STATE EMBLEMS

Cottonwood

Western Meadowlark

Goldenrod

Nevada

One of the world's tallest dams, Hoover Dam, is on the Colorado River at the Nevada–Arizona border. The dam provides flood control, hydroelectric power, and drinking and irrigation water to places as far away as southern California. It has also created Lake Mead, the largest reservoir in the United States.

Gambling is legal in Nevada, and many tourists flock to the state's casinos and hotels to try their luck. Many Nevadans have found jobs in the casinos and hotels. More than 80 percent of the population lives in or near the two principal gambling centers—Las Vegas and the Reno-Lake Tahoe areas.

There are other things that draw visitors to Nevada. People can enjoy outdoor sports at Lake Tahoe, and they can see beautiful desert scenery in Nevada.

Because of its dry climate and desolate terrain, Nevada was one of the last regions in the United States to be explored and settled by people moving westward. Major lodes of silver and gold were discovered in the mid 1800s; as a result, the population increased sixfold between 1860 and 1870. In the 1930s, the state government saw the need to boost the economy. It therefore legalized gambling.

Most of Nevada is within the Great Basin, a desert region. The climate is dry and sunny year-round.

Las Vegas is one of the few cities in the United States where gambling is legal. Las Vegas, known worldwide for its neon lights, casinos, and entertainment, is surrounded by desert. Las Vegas has the largest population of any city in Nevada.

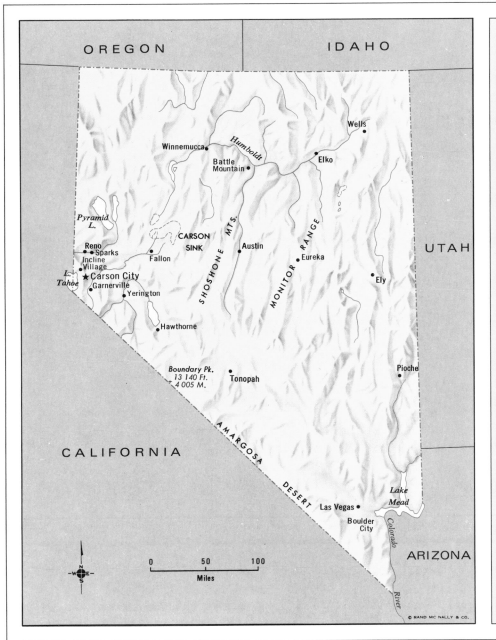

OREGON

IDAHO

Wells

Winnemucca

Humboldt

Battle
Mountain

Elko

*Pyramid
L.*

CARSON
SINK

Austin

MONITOR RANGE

SHOSHONE MTS.

Eureka

UTAH

Reno
Sparks
Incline
Village
Carson City
Garnerville

Fallon

Ely

*L.
Tahoe*

Yerington

Hawthorne

*Boundary Pk.
13 140 Ft.
4 005 M.*

Tonopah

Pioche

CALIFORNIA

*AMARGOSA
DESERT*

*Lake
Mead*

Las Vegas

Boulder
City

Colorado

ARIZONA

River

N
W E
S

0   50   100
Miles

© RAND MC NALLY & CO.

NEVADA

Capital
Carson City (42,500 people)

Area
109,806 square miles
(284,398 sq. km.) Rank: 7th

Population
1,415,400 people Rank: 38th

Statehood
Oct. 31, 1864 (36th state
admitted)

Principal rivers
Colorado River, Humboldt
River

Highest point
Boundary Peak; 13,140 feet
(4,005 m.)

Largest city
Las Vegas (317,900 people)

Motto
All for our country

Song
"Home Means Nevada"

Famous people
Patrick A. McCarran, Howard
R. Hughes, William M.
Stewart, George Wingfield,
Wovoka

STATE EMBLEMS

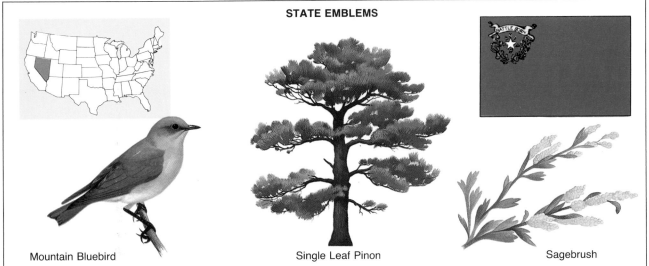

Mountain Bluebird

Single Leaf Pinon

Sagebrush

New Hampshire

The White Mountains of New Hampshire, shown here, contain Mount Washington, the highest peak in the northeastern United States. They also contain a famous landmark known as the Old Man of the Mountain—a natural rock formation that looks like a human face.

More than 85 percent of New Hampshire is covered with forests. The mountainous, wooded landscape brings many vacationers to New Hampshire each year, and the tourism industry these visitors have created employs many New Hampshirites. The climate features short, mild summers and cold winters with heavy snowfall that attracts skiers.

New Hampshire's factories produce electric and electronic goods as well as paper and wood products. Dairy and poultry farms are found in the southern part of the state, and apples, corn, and potatoes are also raised.

Ancestors of American Indians lived in New Hampshire approximately ten thousand years ago. About four thousand Indians were living in New Hampshire when the English began settlement in 1623. In December, 1774, a group of New Hampshirites took over a British fort—an action that contributed to the outbreak of the American Revolution. In 1776, the state adopted its own constitution and thereby became the first colony to be independent from Britain.

Though better known for its mountains, New Hampshire also offers plenty of water. Along the Atlantic Ocean are eighteen miles (twenty-nine kilometers) of beach. Across the state is a belt of freshwater lakes, the largest of which is Lake Winnipesaukee.

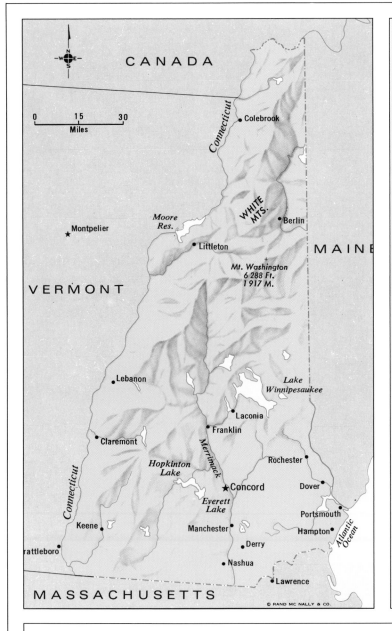

NEW HAMPSHIRE

Capital
Concord (35,800 people)

Area
8,969 square miles (23,230 sq. km.)
Rank: 44th

Population
1,130,000 people Rank: 41st

Statehood
June 21, 1788 (9th state admitted)

Principal rivers
Connecticut River, Merrimack River

Highest point
Mount Washington; 6,288 feet (1,917 m.)

Largest city
Manchester (96,800 people)

Motto
Live free or die

Song
"Old New Hampshire"

Famous people
Mary Baker Eddy, Robert Frost, Horace Greeley, Franklin Pierce, Alan B. Shepard, Jr., Daniel Webster

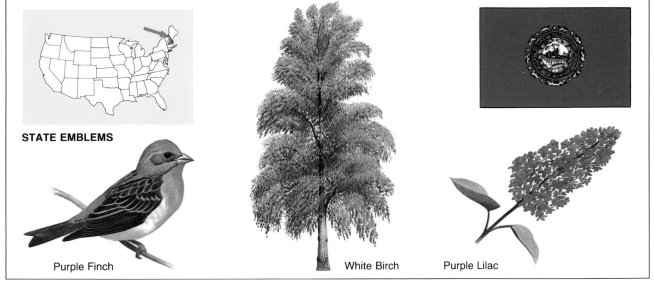

STATE EMBLEMS

Purple Finch

White Birch

Purple Lilac

New Jersey

New Jersey is the most densely populated and urbanized state in the union. Yet, many New Jerseyans live near New York City or Philadelphia, and nearly two-thirds of the state is open land, with farms, forests, salt marshes, and beaches.

New Jersey's eastern beaches bring tourists during the warm summer months. Legalized gambling at Atlantic City is popular. The mountainous western region is snowy in winter and draws skiers.

New Jersey's economy is diverse—neither manufacturing nor farming nor any other area stands out as the most important. Among other things, workers in New Jersey produce chemicals and pharmaceuticals. Farmers raise chickens and dairy cows.

Indians were living in villages in the region when Europeans settled the area in the early 1600s. During the American Revolution, many important battles were fought in New Jersey. In the late 1960s, destructive riots occurred in the cities of New Jersey.

Situated at the edge of the New York City area is Great Swamp National Wildlife Refuge. The refuge is a valuable wilderness area, filled with birds, mammals, reptiles, and other animals. It is threatened, however, by pollution and intrusion from nearby cities.

Thomas Edison was one of the greatest inventors of all time. His more than one thousand inventions included the electric light bulb, the phonograph, and the motion picture camera. He set up several laboratories in New Jersey, one of which is shown here.

NEW JERSEY • 69

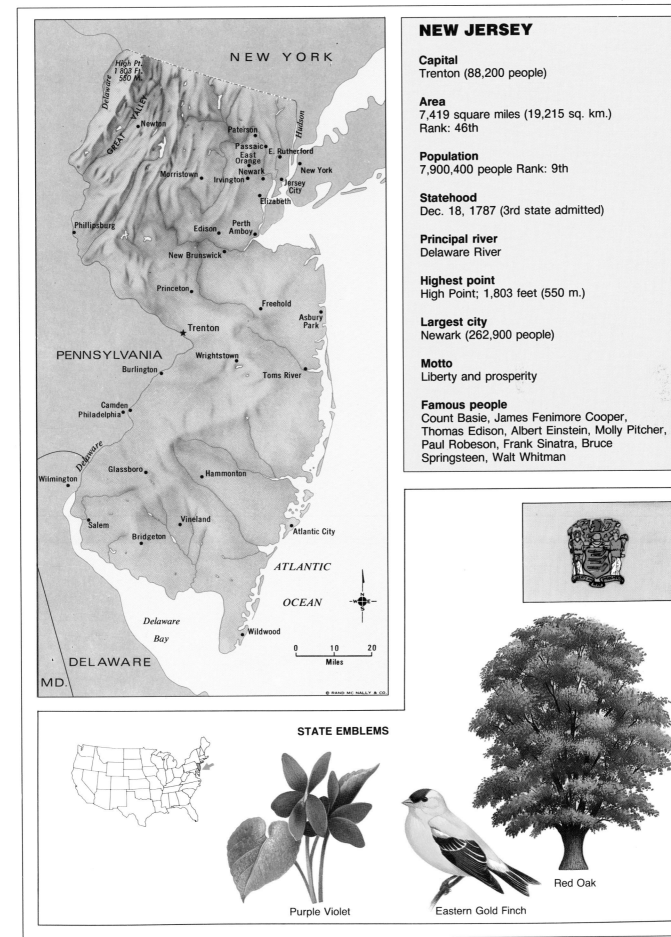

NEW JERSEY

Capital
Trenton (88,200 people)

Area
7,419 square miles (19,215 sq. km.)
Rank: 46th

Population
7,900,400 people Rank: 9th

Statehood
Dec. 18, 1787 (3rd state admitted)

Principal river
Delaware River

Highest point
High Point; 1,803 feet (550 m.)

Largest city
Newark (262,900 people)

Motto
Liberty and prosperity

Famous people
Count Basie, James Fenimore Cooper, Thomas Edison, Albert Einstein, Molly Pitcher, Paul Robeson, Frank Sinatra, Bruce Springsteen, Walt Whitman

STATE EMBLEMS

Purple Violet

Eastern Gold Finch

Red Oak

New Mexico

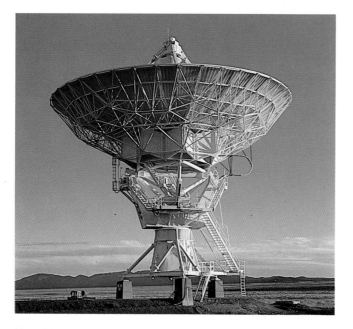

New Mexico plays a big role in scientific discovery. From the flat Plains of San Agustin, scientists observe the sun or distant planets. Pictured is a type of telescope that allows astronomers to view stars and other regions in the galaxy never seen before.

Ancestors of American Indians first lived in what is now New Mexico about twenty thousand years ago. The cultures of these people and their descendants were among the most sophisticated of all Indian societies in North America. Among their discoveries were methods of conserving water, a precious commodity in dry New Mexico. The Spanish settled in New Mexico in the 1500s and 1600s. The region was part of Mexico before it entered the United States.

Mining is important in New Mexico. The state has significant reserves of oil, natural gas, copper, and uranium. The United States government employs many New Mexicans. Farmers on the eastern plains raise cattle and sheep.

New Mexico's beautiful landscape includes deserts, mountains, and plains. Its climate features much sunshine, low humidity, and warm winter temperatures. And its culture blends Indian, Spanish, and American influences. These factors combine to draw many tourists to New Mexico.

The remarkable caves at Carlsbad Caverns National Park extend more than twenty miles (thirty-five kilometers) and reach depths of 1,100 feet (335 meters). In summer, visitors can view the spectacular sight of thousands of bats who live in the caves flying out into the night.

NEW MEXICO

Capital
Santa Fe (60,300 people)

Area
121,364 square miles
(314,333 sq. km.) Rank: 5th

Population
1,624,500 people
Rank: 36th

Statehood
Jan. 6, 1912 (47th state
admitted)

Principal rivers
Rio Grande, Pecos River

Highest point
Wheeler Peak; 13,161 feet
(4,011 m.)

Largest city
Albuquerque (416,500
people)

Motto
Crescit eundo (It grows as
it goes)

Song
"Asi es Nuevo Mexico" and
"O, Fair New Mexico"

Famous people
Kit Carson, Georgia
O'Keefe, Jean Baptiste
Lamy

STATE EMBLEMS

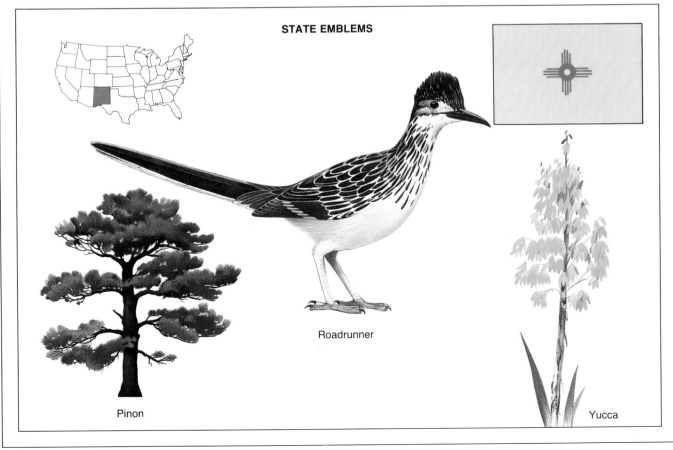

Pinon

Roadrunner

Yucca

New York

Niagara Falls is on the Niagara River between Ontario, Canada, and western New York. This world-famous landmark draws thousands of tourists each year and generates much hydroelectric power. It is actually two falls, and the larger is more than five blocks across.

New York City is the most populous city in the United States and in the top five worldwide. The Big Apple—the city's nickname—has unlimited sights to offer visitors. Among them is the Statue of Liberty, given to the United States by France in 1886.

New York is the second most populous state in the country, after California. Most New Yorkers live in or near New York City, one of the largest cities in the world. Tourists come from all over the world to see New York City and to enjoy its professional sports teams, theaters, restaurants, and other cultural attractions.

But other areas of New York attract people with their natural beauty. New York's terrain includes the Adirondack and Catskill mountains and shoreline on Lakes Erie and Ontario. Ocean coastline on Long Island includes magnificent beaches.

Southern New York's climate is cool in the winter and hot in the summer. In the north and west, the summers are shorter, and the winters, colder.

In the 1620s, the Dutch established colonies on Manhattan Island, which they bought from Indians for the equivalent of twenty-four dollars. About one-third of the major battles of the American Revolution were fought on New York soil.

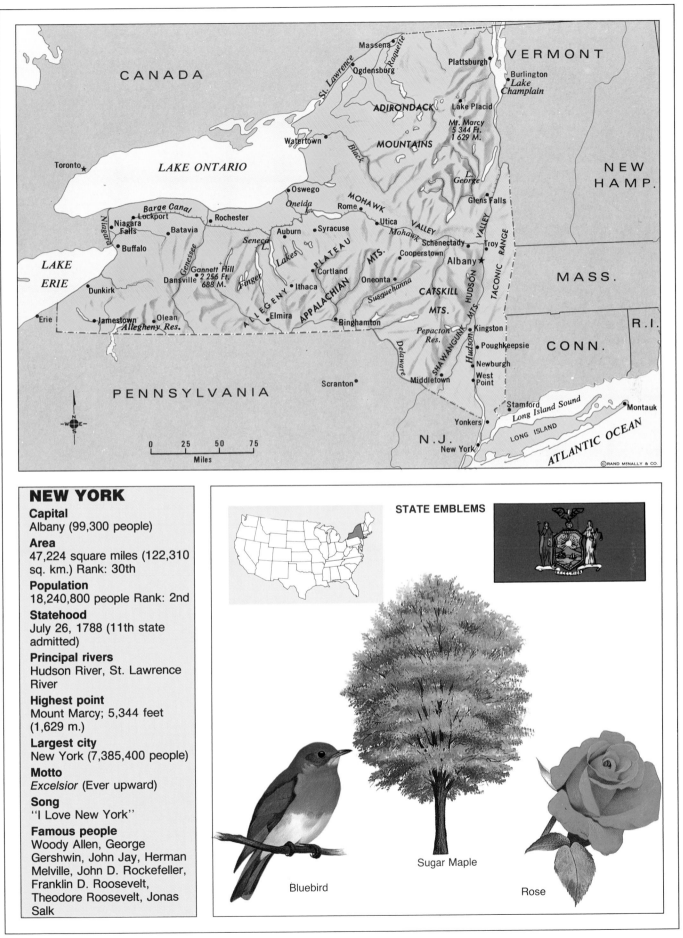

NEW YORK

Capital
Albany (99,300 people)

Area
47,224 square miles (122,310 sq. km.) Rank: 30th

Population
18,240,800 people Rank: 2nd

Statehood
July 26, 1788 (11th state admitted)

Principal rivers
Hudson River, St. Lawrence River

Highest point
Mount Marcy; 5,344 feet (1,629 m.)

Largest city
New York (7,385,400 people)

Motto
Excelsior (Ever upward)

Song
"I Love New York"

Famous people
Woody Allen, George Gershwin, John Jay, Herman Melville, John D. Rockefeller, Franklin D. Roosevelt, Theodore Roosevelt, Jonas Salk

STATE EMBLEMS

Bluebird

Sugar Maple

Rose

North Carolina

The Outer Banks are islands off the coast of North Carolina that protect the mainland from severe winds and wave erosion brought on by the Atlantic Ocean. Several small fishing villages are found on the islands, as well as two national seashores.

N o one knows what happened to the colony at Roanoke Island. The island, which lies off North Carolina's coast, was the site of the first English settlement in the Americas. After several unsuccessful attempts at setting up a permanent colony, it seemed to the English that they had succeeded in 1587. In 1590, however, visitors to the colony found the buildings deserted and in ruins. To this day, the fate of the colony at Roanoke remains a mystery. In summer, visitors to the island can watch an outdoor drama that recreates the story of the colony.

North Carolina was the site of another historic first: the first airplane flight. In the early 1900s, Wilbur and Orville Wright conducted their aviation experiments at Kitty Hawk. To honor the Wright Brothers, a national monument now stands at Kitty Hawk.

North Carolinians make textiles, cigarettes, and furniture. More tobacco is grown here than in any other state.

Summers are hot and winters are mild in the east, with cooler temperatures in the west.

Great Smoky Mountains National Park straddles the border of Tennessee and North Carolina. The Great Smoky Mountains, part of the Appalachian Mountains, were named for the bluish haze that covers them. The haze is the result of hydrocarbons released by conifer trees.

NORTH CAROLINA

Capital
Raleigh (225,700 people)

Area
48,718 square miles (126,180 sq. km.) Rank: 29th

Population
6,992,300 people Rank: 10th

Statehood
Nov. 21, 1789 (12th state admitted)

Principal rivers
Roanoke River, Neuse River, Cape Fear River

Highest point
Mount Mitchell; 6,684 feet (2,037 m.)

Largest city
Charlotte (462,700 people)

Motto
Esse quam videri (To be rather than to seem)

Song
"The Old North State"

Famous people
Virginia Dare, Billy Graham, Andrew Johnson, Dolley Madison, James K. Polk, Wilbur and Orville Wright

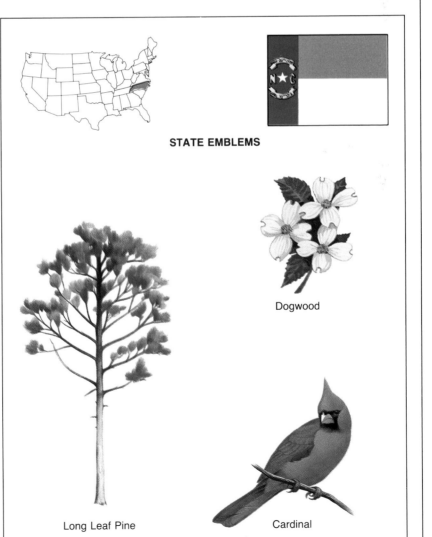

STATE EMBLEMS

Dogwood

Long Leaf Pine

Cardinal

North Dakota

In the southwest corner of North Dakota lie the Badlands, which were named because early travelers found the region difficult to cross. The Badlands were formed by sandstone, shale, and clay. Many prehistoric fossils have been found here.

The days of the Old West are recreated at Medora, North Dakota. The former cattle town was established 1883, and it is situated in the western part of the state, near the south unit of Theodore Roosevelt National Park. Shown here is a scene from the Medora Musical.

North Dakota possesses a challenging climate with long, cold winters and short, hot summers that bring little moisture to support crops. But after railroads first reached North Dakota in the 1870s, settlers rushed into the territory, eager to farm the prairie despite the severe weather. Through trial and error, North Dakotans developed methods of cultivation suited for the dry climate and short growing season. Today, North Dakota produces more wheat than any other state except Kansas.

Among the Indians early settlers encountered in North Dakota were the Sioux, who did not want to give up their lands. Settlement west and north of the Missouri River was hindered by the Sioux until 1881, when Sitting Bull, a brave Sioux leader, surrendered to the United States.

Two different plains regions with different geologic histories meet in North Dakota: the Great Plains lie in the west, and the plains that form the southern and western Great Lakes region are found in the east.

NORTH DAKOTA

Capital
Bismarck (51,800 people)

Area
68,994 square miles (178,694 sq. km.)
Rank: 17th

Population
636,000 people
Rank: 47th

Statehood
Nov. 2, 1889 (39th state admitted)

Principal rivers
Missouri River, Red River

Highest point
White Butte; 3,506 feet (1,069 m.)

Largest city
Fargo (79,200 people)

Motto
Liberty and union, now and forever, one and inseparable

Song
"North Dakota Hymn"

Famous people
Louis L'Amour, Maxwell Anderson, Peggy Lee, Eric Severeid, Lawrence Welk

The valley of the Red River of the North is a rich agricultural region. The river flows north along the North Dakota–Minnesota border into Canada.

STATE EMBLEMS

Wild Prairie Rose

American Elm

Western Meadowlark

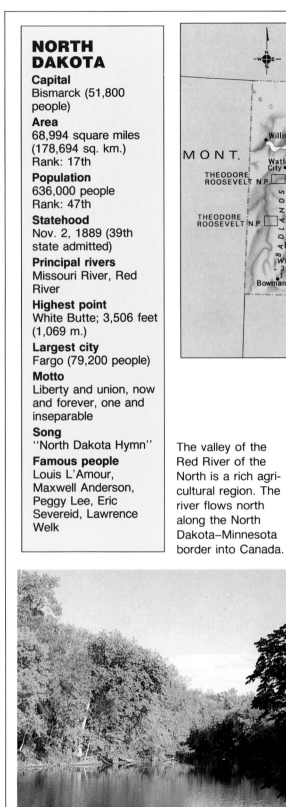

Ohio

The Mound Builders were groups of Indians who lived in what is now called the Midwest. They were called the Mound Builders because they built thousands of earthen burial and ceremonial mounds. Mound Builders lived in Ohio between 1000 B.C. and A.D. 800. Visitors to Ohio can see many of their mounds, some of them with unusual shapes.

Ohio's waterways have been important to its development. Set between the Ohio River and Lake Erie and crossed by roads, railways, and canals, Ohio has been able to take in raw materials from many sources and ship out finished products. Today, Ohio is a leading manufacturing state, ranking third behind California and New York in the value of its manufactured products. Especially important are transportation equipment, rubber products, and machine tools. Ohioans also mine coal and grow corn.

West of the Scioto River is a gently rolling plain. To the east of the river, the land is hillier. It is cold in Ohio in winter, and in summer, it is hot and humid.

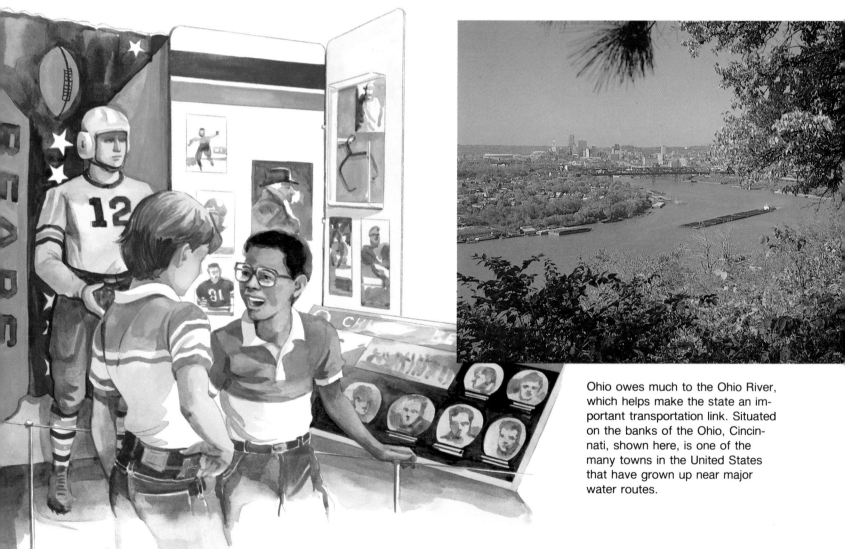

Ohio owes much to the Ohio River, which helps make the state an important transportation link. Situated on the banks of the Ohio, Cincinnati, shown here, is one of the many towns in the United States that have grown up near major water routes.

Some say that football has replaced baseball as the national pastime of the United States. The sport is played at all levels of age and skill, from peewee to professional. The Pro Football Hall of Fame, in Canton, is a museum devoted entirely to professional football's history and heroes.

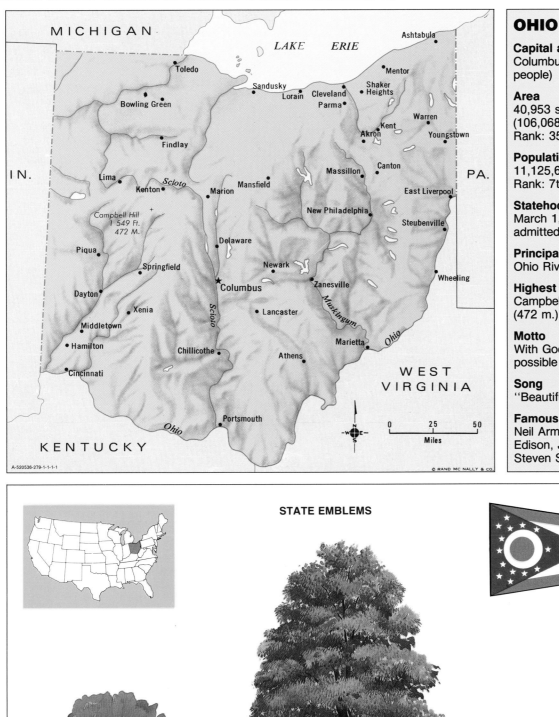

MICHIGAN

LAKE ERIE

Ashtabula

Toledo

Mentor

Sandusky
Lorain   Cleveland   Shaker Heights
Bowling Green   Parma

Warren

Kent
Akron
Youngstown

Findlay

Canton

IN.

Lima
Kenton   *Scioto*   Marion   Mansfield   Massillon   East Liverpool   PA.

New Philadelphia

Steubenville

Campbell Hill
1 549 Ft.
472 M.

Delaware

Piqua

Newark

Springfield

Wheeling

Dayton   Columbus   *Scioto*   Zanesville   *Muskingum*

Xenia

Middletown   Lancaster

Hamilton   Chillicothe   Athens   Marietta   *Ohio*

Cincinnati

WEST
VIRGINIA

Portsmouth

Ohio

KENTUCKY

N
W E
S

0   25   50
Miles

A-520536-279-1-1-1-1   © RAND MC NALLY & CO.

OHIO

Capital and largest city
Columbus (649,700 people)

Area
40,953 square miles (106,068 sq. km.)
Rank: 35th

Population
11,125,600 people
Rank: 7th

Statehood
March 1, 1803 (17th state admitted)

Principal rivers
Ohio River, Scioto River

Highest point
Campbell Hill; 1,549 feet (472 m.)

Motto
With God, all things are possible

Song
"Beautiful Ohio"

Famous people
Neil Armstrong, Thomas Edison, John Glenn, Steven Spielberg

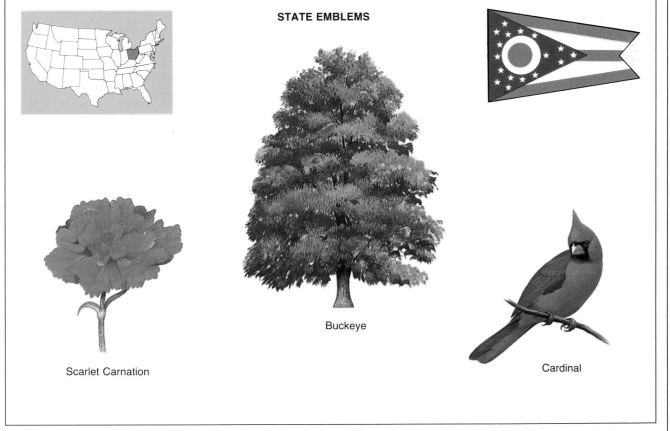

STATE EMBLEMS

Buckeye

Scarlet Carnation

Cardinal

Oklahoma

The area shown here, which lies in Oklahoma's Panhandle, was in the heart of the Dust Bowl of the 1930s. Since that time, conservation practices such as improved farming methods and tree planting have turned the region into a productive area once again.

Oklahoma, once set aside as Indian Territory, was not opened for settlement until about twenty-five years after the Civil War. The subsequent land rush brought thousands of settlers to the state to establish homesteads. They began plowing up the prairie soil to plant crops.

Then, in the 1930s, long droughts occurred. Without the prairie grasses to anchor the dry land, the wind picked up much of the soil, creating dust and sand storms that buried houses and roads. Huge dust clouds were seen hundreds of miles away, and the region became known as the Dust Bowl. More than half of the population moved away.

Today, Oklahomans use better methods of farming to produce wheat and to raise livestock. The mining of oil and natural gas is also significant.

The flat western portion of Oklahoma is part of the Great Plains. Farther east, the land is hilly or mountainous. Oklahoma summers are long and usually very hot. Winters are short but can be very cold.

Although real cowboys work hard at jobs that are often dull and pay little, the myth of the cowboy hero of the Old West lives on. In Oklahoma, people can watch cowboys in action at horse shows and rodeos, and they can visit the National Cowboy Hall of Fame in Oklahoma City.

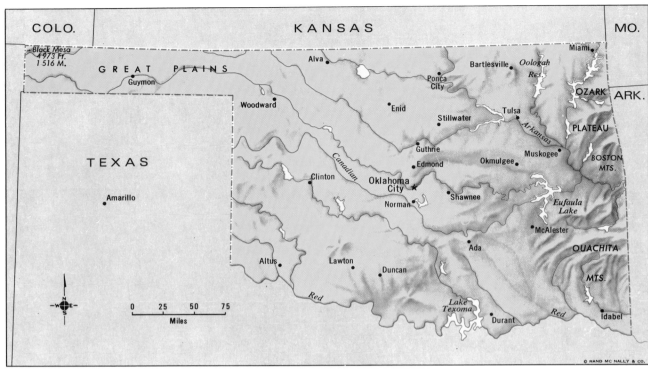

OKLAHOMA

Capital and largest city
Oklahoma City (457,800 people)

Area
68,679 square miles (177,879 sq. km.)
Rank: 19th

Population
3,239,500 people Rank: 28th

Statehood
Nov. 16, 1907 (46th state admitted)

Principal rivers
Arkansas River, Canadian River, Red River

Highest point
Black Mesa; 4,973 feet (1,516 m.)

Motto
Labor omnia vincit (Labor conquers all things)

Song
"Oklahoma"

Famous people
Carl Albert, Woody Guthrie, Lynn Riggs, Oral Roberts, Will Rogers, Maria Tallchief, Jim Thorpe

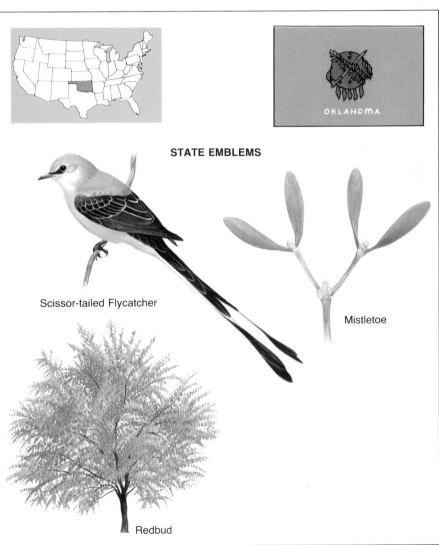

STATE EMBLEMS

Scissor-tailed Flycatcher

Mistletoe

Redbud

Oregon

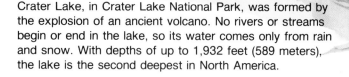

Crater Lake, in Crater Lake National Park, was formed by the explosion of an ancient volcano. No rivers or streams begin or end in the lake, so its water comes only from rain and snow. With depths of up to 1,932 feet (589 meters), the lake is the second deepest in North America.

Rising steeply from the Pacific Ocean, Oregon's coast is typical of much of the Northwest. Moisture from the Pacific drops here and helps agriculture and forests. The rugged, irregular coastline adds beauty and features protected areas for use as ports.

The Cascade Range divides Oregon into a humid, fertile west and a drier east. Winds from the west pick up moisture from the Pacific Ocean. As the air rises to cross the mountains, it cools and drops its moisture in the form of rain or snow. The Cascade Range, therefore, receives much precipitation, and the regions to the east remain dry.

Nearly half the state is covered with dense forests, and many Oregonians are involved in wood industries. They cut down trees and make lumber, plywood, and paper. Most people live in the Willamette Valley, between the Coast and Cascade ranges. Here fruits and vegetables are grown. In the east, ranching and grazing are dominant.

Oregon is a beautiful state, and its parks and recreation areas attract many visitors. People come to Oregon to hike, camp, ski, and enjoy other outdoor activities.

The first explorers to come to Oregon by land were the members of the Lewis and Clark Expedition in 1805. Settlers began coming to the area in the 1830s.

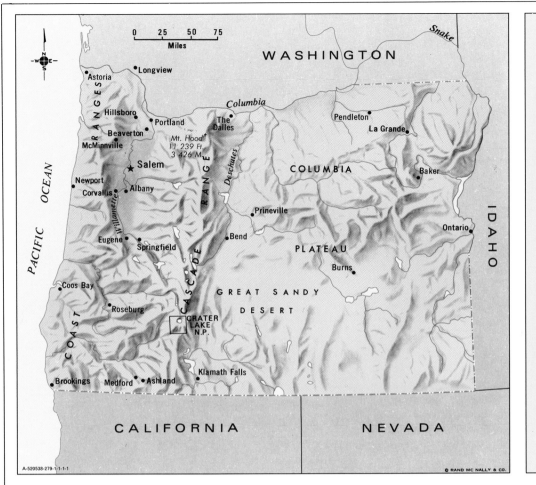

OREGON

Capital
Salem (115,500 people)

Area
96,002 square miles
(248,645 sq. km.)
Rank: 10th

Population
3,062,000 people
Rank: 29th

Statehood
Feb. 14, 1859 (33rd state admitted)

Principal river
Columbia River

Highest point
Mount Hood; 11,239 feet (3,426 m.)

Largest city
Portland (458,400 people)

Motto
The Union

Song
"Oregon, My Oregon"

Famous people
Robert Gray, Chief Joseph, Linus Pauling

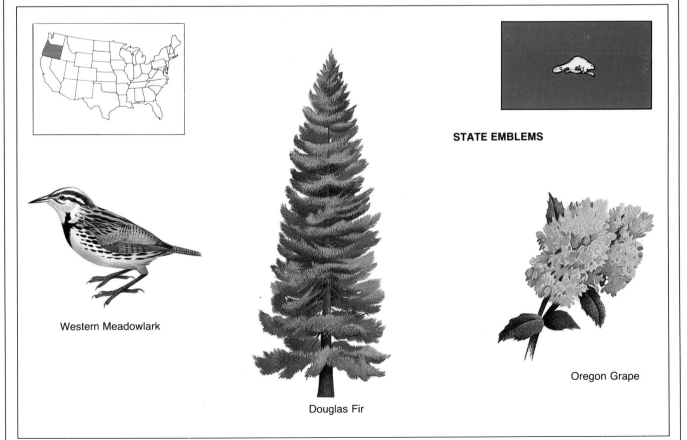

STATE EMBLEMS

Western Meadowlark

Douglas Fir

Oregon Grape

Pennsylvania

Pennsylvania occupies a key position in several ways. It was at the center of the thirteen original states. It links the East with the Midwest. And Pennsylvania's cities have played key roles in history. Philadelphia, once the largest city in North America, was especially prominent in the early days of the United States, while Pittsburgh has been vital to industry in the nineteenth and twentieth centuries.

Among the earliest Pennsylvanians were the Quakers, who were members of a religious group that came from Great Britain in the 1680s. German settlers who came later still live in the state, and today they are known as the Pennsylvania Dutch.

Much of Pennsylvania's terrain is formed by the Appalachians and the Allegheny Plateau, where summers are cool and winter snowfalls are heavy. Lower areas are warmer.

The coal, steel, and oil industries have been important in Pennsylvania for many years. Pennsylvania is one of the country's leading manufacturing states.

The lush green landscape of Pennsylvania, shown here, is the result of careful farming and conservation methods. Farmers in the state have practiced crop rotation, which keeps the soil productive. Forests that were once nearly wiped out have been restored and now thrive.

In the early battles of the Civil War, the South gained several important wins. At Gettysburg, Pennsylvania, in July, 1863, the Confederacy suffered a major loss. This bloody battle is now considered the turning point of the war for the North, which eventually won the war.

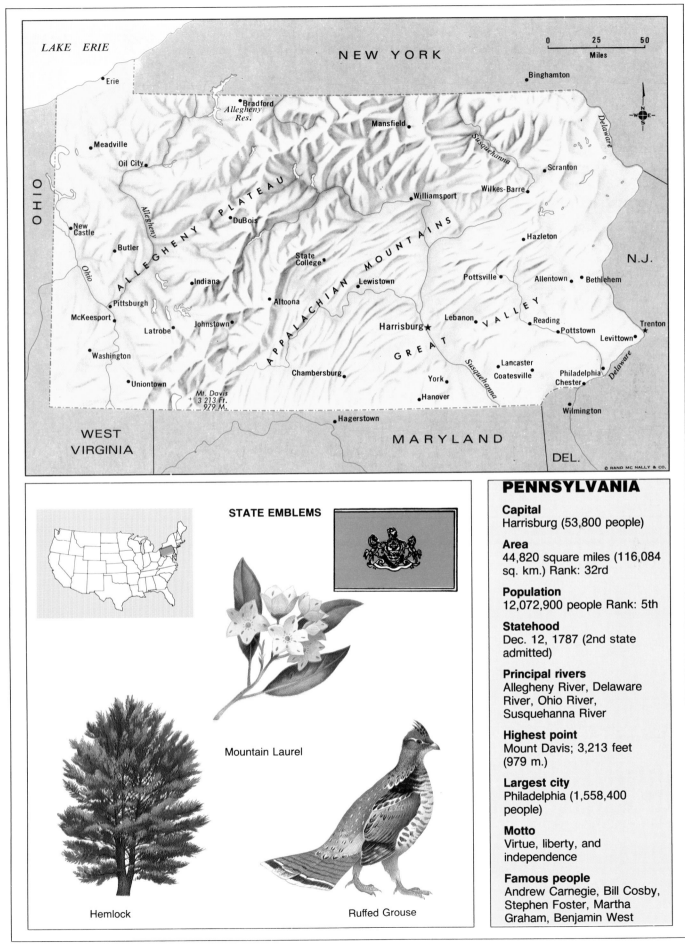

LAKE ERIE

NEW YORK

0   25   50
Miles

Erie

Binghamton

Bradford
Allegheny Res.

Mansfield

Delaware

Susquehanna

Meadville

Oil City

Scranton

Wilkes-Barre

Williamsport

ALLEGHENY PLATEAU

DuBois

New Castle

Hazleton

Butler

State College

APPALACHIAN MOUNTAINS

N.J.

Indiana

Lewistown

Pottsville

Allentown

Bethlehem

Allegheny

Altoona

VALLEY

Pittsburgh

Lebanon

Reading

Pottstown

Trenton

Ohio

McKeesport

Latrobe

Johnstown

Harrisburg ★

GREAT

Levittown

Washington

Lancaster

Coatesville

Philadelphia

Chester

Delaware

Chambersburg

York

Susquehanna

Uniontown

Mt. Davis
+ 3,213 Ft.
979 M.

Hanover

Wilmington

OHIO

WEST VIRGINIA

Hagerstown

MARYLAND

DEL.

© RAND MC NALLY & CO.

STATE EMBLEMS

Mountain Laurel

Hemlock

Ruffed Grouse

PENNSYLVANIA

Capital
Harrisburg (53,800 people)

Area
44,820 square miles (116,084 sq. km.) Rank: 32rd

Population
12,072,900 people Rank: 5th

Statehood
Dec. 12, 1787 (2nd state admitted)

Principal rivers
Allegheny River, Delaware River, Ohio River, Susquehanna River

Highest point
Mount Davis; 3,213 feet (979 m.)

Largest city
Philadelphia (1,558,400 people)

Motto
Virtue, liberty, and independence

Famous people
Andrew Carnegie, Bill Cosby, Stephen Foster, Martha Graham, Benjamin West

Rhode Island

In warm months, boating, sailing, and fishing tournaments abound in Rhode Island. One of the most famous of all sailboat races, the America's Cup, was held off Newport for many years. Here, young sailors enjoy their sport at Block Island.

Rhode Island is the smallest state. At its broadest point, it is less than fifty miles (eighty kilometers) wide. The eastern part of the state includes many islands and is gently rolling. The western part is hilly and rocky. Because Rhode Island is right on the ocean, its weather is mild.

A large percentage of all workers in Rhode Island are involved in activities such as insurance, printing and publishing, and trade. More than 80 percent of all Rhode Islanders live in urban areas—one of the highest percentages of urban dwellers in the country.

In the summer, vacationers can swim, sail, or fish in Narragansett Bay, Rhode Island Sound, and Block Island Sound.

English colonists from Massachusetts came to Rhode Island in the 1630s and established the first permanent settlements. Rhode Island declared independence from England on May 4, 1776. It was the first colony to do so. The first factory in the United States was built in Rhode Island in the 1790s.

In the late 1800s, Newport, Rhode Island, became a fashionable resort for the rich. Many of the huge Newport mansions built by the wealthy families are now museums. One of the most famous is the Breakers, a seventy-room mansion owned by the Vanderbilt family.

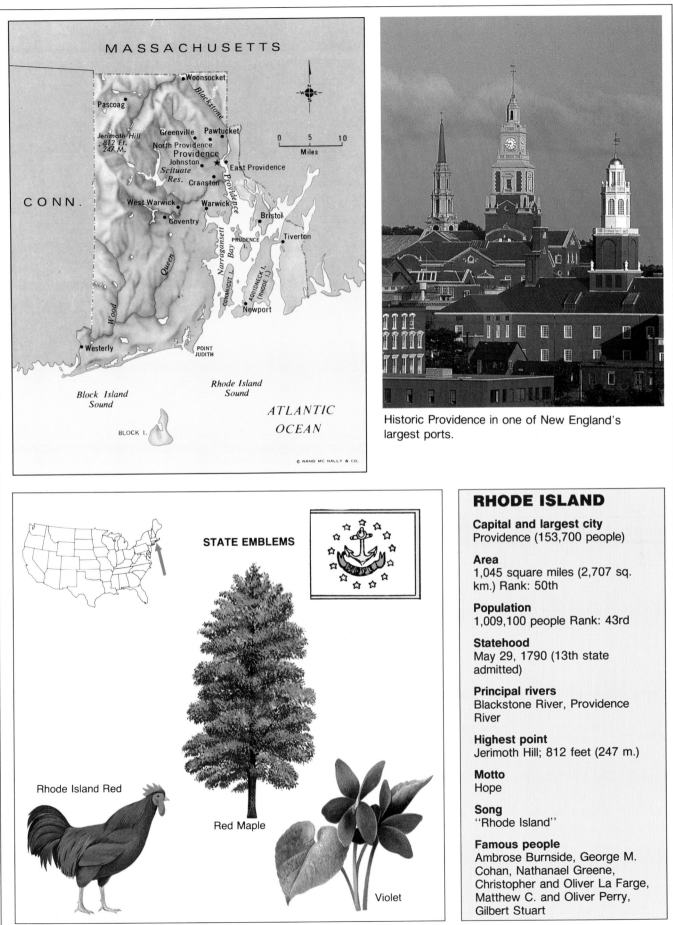

MASSACHUSETTS

Woonsocket

Pascoag

Blackstone

Jerimoth Hill
812 Ft.
247 M.

Greenville   Pawtucket
North Providence
Providence
Johnston   East Providence
Scituate
Res.   Cranston

CONN.

West Warwick   Warwick

Coventry

Narragansett Bay   PRUDENCE I.

Bristol

Tiverton

CONANICUT I.

AQUIDNECK I.
(RHODE I.)

Queen

Wood

Newport

Westerly   POINT
JUDITH

Block Island
Sound

Rhode Island
Sound

BLOCK I.

ATLANTIC
OCEAN

0   5   10
Miles

© RAND MC NALLY & CO.

Historic Providence in one of New England's largest ports.

STATE EMBLEMS

Rhode Island Red

Red Maple

Violet

RHODE ISLAND

Capital and largest city
Providence (153,700 people)

Area
1,045 square miles (2,707 sq. km.) Rank: 50th

Population
1,009,100 people Rank: 43rd

Statehood
May 29, 1790 (13th state admitted)

Principal rivers
Blackstone River, Providence River

Highest point
Jerimoth Hill; 812 feet (247 m.)

Motto
Hope

Song
"Rhode Island"

Famous people
Ambrose Burnside, George M. Cohan, Nathanael Greene, Christopher and Oliver La Farge, Matthew C. and Oliver Perry, Gilbert Stuart

South Carolina

Founded in 1670, Charleston is South Carolina's oldest city and one of the most historic cities in the country. Many carefully preserved buildings line the streets of Charleston, and today, they are reminders of the state's southern heritage.

After the American Revolution, South Carolina became a land of prosperous cotton plantations. These plantations depended on slaves from Africa who worked them. The question of whether the United States should allow slavery was central to the issues of the Civil War. Since South Carolina's economy depended on this source of labor, it fought on the side that was for slavery, the South. The war started at Fort Sumter, situated in Charleston Harbor. South Carolina's economy suffered after the South lost the war, as did the economies of other southern states.

Cotton is still grown in South Carolina, but tobacco and soybeans are more important. A big business today in South Carolina is the making of cotton cloth, or *textiles*. South Carolinians also produce chemicals, machinery, and electrical equipment.

The land along the coast, nicknamed the Low Country, is flat. Inland, in the Up Country, it is hillier, and in the northwest, mountainous. The climate is humid, with long, hot summers and short, mild winters.

The Grand Strand is a fifty-mile (eighty-kilometer) stretch of beach that lies on the Atlantic Ocean near the North Carolina border. This is an area that brings many visitors interested in seaside vacations. Myrtle Beach is especially popular.

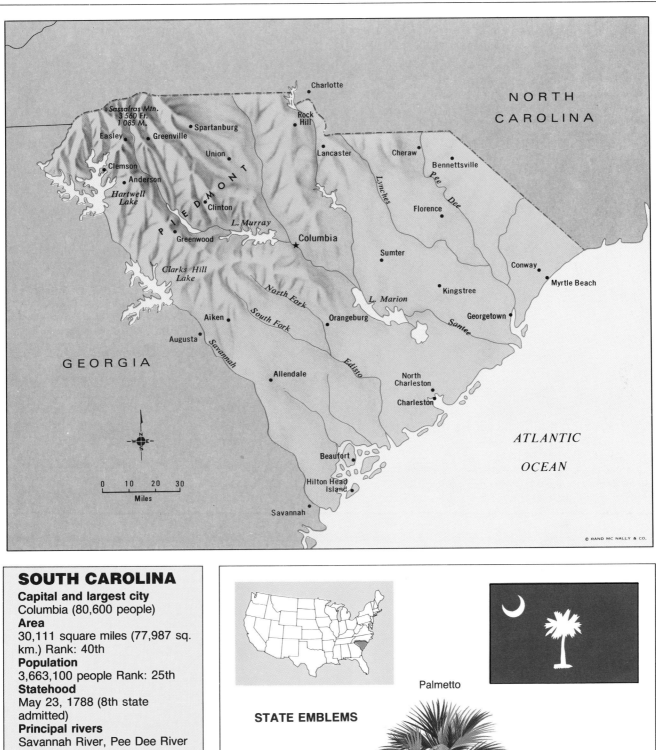

Charlotte

NORTH CAROLINA

Sassafras Mtn.
3,560 Ft.
1,085 M.

Rock Hill

Spartanburg

Easley • Greenville

Union

Lancaster

Cheraw

Bennettsville

Clemson

Anderson

Hartwell Lake

P I E D M O N T

Clinton

L. Murray

Florence

Pee Dee

Lynches

Greenwood

Columbia

Sumter

Clarks Hill Lake

Conway

Myrtle Beach

North Fork

L. Marion

Kingstree

Georgetown

Aiken

South Fork

Orangeburg

Santee

Augusta

Savannah

GEORGIA

Allendale

Edisto

North Charleston

Charleston

ATLANTIC

OCEAN

Beaufort

Hilton Head Island

Savannah

0 10 20 30
Miles

© RAND MC NALLY & CO.

SOUTH CAROLINA

Capital and largest city
Columbia (80,600 people)
Area
30,111 square miles (77,987 sq. km.) Rank: 40th
Population
3,663,100 people Rank: 25th
Statehood
May 23, 1788 (8th state admitted)
Principal rivers
Savannah River, Pee Dee River
Highest point
Sassafras Mountain; 3,560 feet (1,085 m.)
Motto
Animis opibusque parati (Prepared in mind and resources) and *Dum spiro spero* (While I breathe, I hope)
Song
"South Carolina on My Mind"
Famous people
Mary McLeod Bethune, John C. Calhoun, Robert Mills

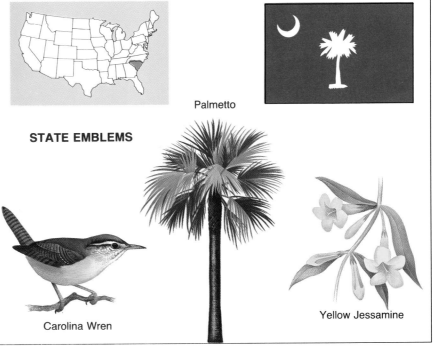

Palmetto

STATE EMBLEMS

Yellow Jessamine

Carolina Wren

South Dakota

Situated in the Black Hills is Mount Rushmore, a sixty-foot (eighteen-meter) sculpture of the heads of four United States presidents. The presidents are, from left to right, George Washington, Thomas Jefferson, Theodore Roosevelt, and Abraham Lincoln.

South Dakota's dams and reservoirs have helped the state by serving as sources of hydroelectric power, flood control, and irrigation. Making more water available for irrigation and livestock is important, as agriculture plays a major role in the state's economy.

In the southwest corner of South Dakota lie the Black Hills. They look black from a distance because they are covered with thick pine forests. These hills attract visitors who are interested in outdoor recreation.

South Dakota's farmers either raise livestock or grow corn, wheat, or hay. The nation's largest gold mine is in South Dakota. The majority of South Dakotans live in rural areas—on farms or in small towns.

Indians inhabited the region for thousands of years before French explorers arrived in the 1740s. Many settlers came in the 1870s, after hearing news of the discovery of gold in the Black Hills. They occupied lands that had been promised to the Indians, and many battles were fought as a result. The Indians were finally forced to live on reservations.

Glaciers that once covered eastern South Dakota left behind good land for farming. The Great Plains make up the western part of the state. This region is mostly dry, treeless, grassland. South Dakota has hot summers and very cold winters.

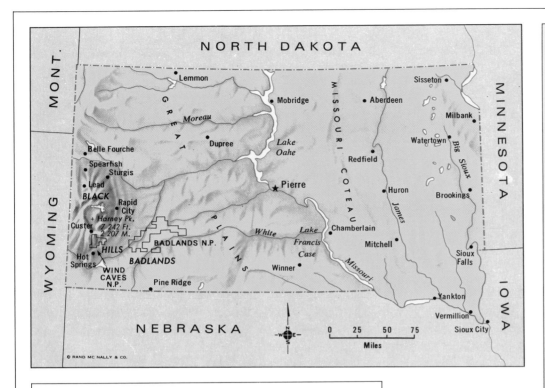

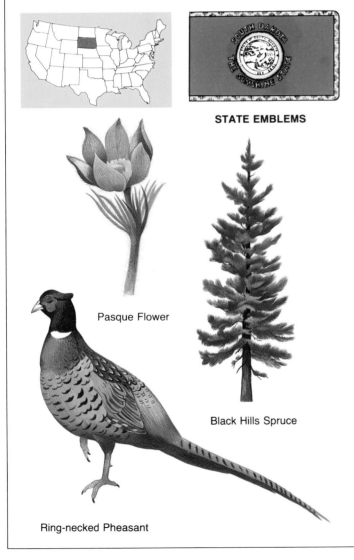

STATE EMBLEMS

Pasque Flower

Black Hills Spruce

Ring-necked Pheasant

SOUTH DAKOTA

Capital
Pierre (13,400 people)

Area
75,896 square miles
(196,571 sq. km.)
Rank: 16th

Population
717,500 people
Rank: 45th

Statehood
Nov. 2, 1889 (40th
state admitted)

Principal rivers
James River, Missouri
River

Highest point
Harney Peak; 7,242
feet (2,207 m.)

Largest city
Sioux Falls (106,400
people)

Motto
Under God the people
rule

Song
"Hail, South Dakota"

Famous people
Sitting Bull, Pierre
Chouteau, Jr., Crazy
Horse, Calamity Jane,
George McGovern,
Laura Ingalls Wilder

The Badlands of
southwestern South
Dakota is a region of
unusual rock forma-
tions created by
erosion.

Tennessee

In 1541, Spanish explorers who crossed Tennessee were the first Europeans to see the Mississippi River, near the site of present-day Memphis. Tennessee was divided on the issues of the Civil War, but eventually it sided with the South. Because of its location at the North-South border, more Civil War battles were fought in Tennessee than in any other state except Virginia. The history of Tennessee can be glimpsed at several sites around the state.

Tennessee's beautiful terrain also draws tourists. It ranges from mountains in the east to floodplains along the river in the west. Near the middle is the Cumberland Plateau, a high, hilly region. Great Smoky Mountains National park is one of the most popular national parks in the country. Summers are hot, and winters are generally short and mild.

Factory workers in Tennessee produce textiles, metals, and chemicals, while Tennessean miners dig for coal, zinc, and other minerals.

Great Smoky Mountain National Park is the largest and best known park in Tennessee. Clingmans Dome, the highest point in the state, is found in this park. Pictured here are the Great Smoky Mountains, which are named for the bluish haze that normally covers them.

Nashville a world center for country music. The Grand Old Opry, which started as a radio show in the 1920s, has had much to do with country music's history and growth. Today, Opryland is a major concert center on the outskirts of Nashville.

TENNESSEE

Capital
Nashville (502,800 people)

Area
41,219 square miles (106,757 sq. km.)
Rank: 34th

Population
5,112,800 people Rank: 17th

Statehood
June 1, 1796 (16th state admitted)

Principal rivers
Mississippi River, Tennessee River

Highest point
Clingmans Dome; 6,643 feet (2,025 m.)

Largest city
Memphis (626,700 people)

Motto
Agriculture and commerce

Song
"The Tennessee Waltz" and four others

Famous people
Davy Crockett, Dolly Parton

The Civil War cannon shown here overlooks Chattanooga at the Moccasin Bend of the Tennessee River.

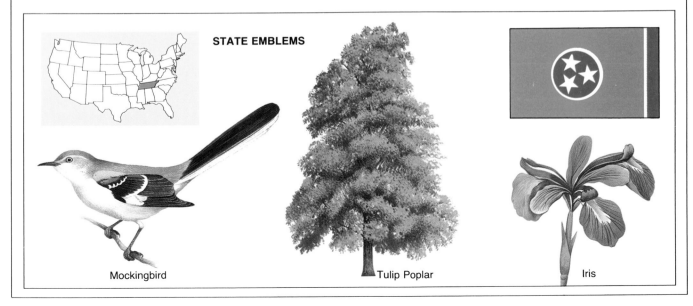

STATE EMBLEMS

Mockingbird

Tulip Poplar

Iris

Texas

Texas is home to some of the busiest and biggest cities in the United States, but it is also a land of huge farms and ranches. Agriculture is still a major industry, and the High Plains region in the Texas Panhandle, shown here, contains productive farmland.

Texas fought for independence from Mexico in the 1830s. In 1836, about two hundred Texans withdrew into an old Spanish mission in San Antonio called the Alamo, shown here. They fought off more than five thousand Mexicans for almost two weeks, but the Mexicans eventually won the battle.

When Mexico gained independence from Spain in 1821, the land that is now Texas was part of Mexico. Texas broke free from Mexico in the 1830s, and for a time, it was an independent republic.

After the Civil War, cattle ranching became important in Texas. In 1901, a great oil gusher was discovered, and soon oil was found all over the state. Drilling for oil remains a major business in Texas, although cattle ranching is still very important. The largest cattle ranch in the country, which is about as big as the state of Rhode Island, is in Texas. Texans also grow cotton, wheat, and fruits.

Texas is the third most populous state and the second largest state. Because it is so big, it includes different types of land, from coastal plains in the east to the Great Plains in the northwest to mountains west of the Pecos River. In the east and along the coast, there are mild winters and hot, humid summers. In the west, the winters are colder, and it is very dry.

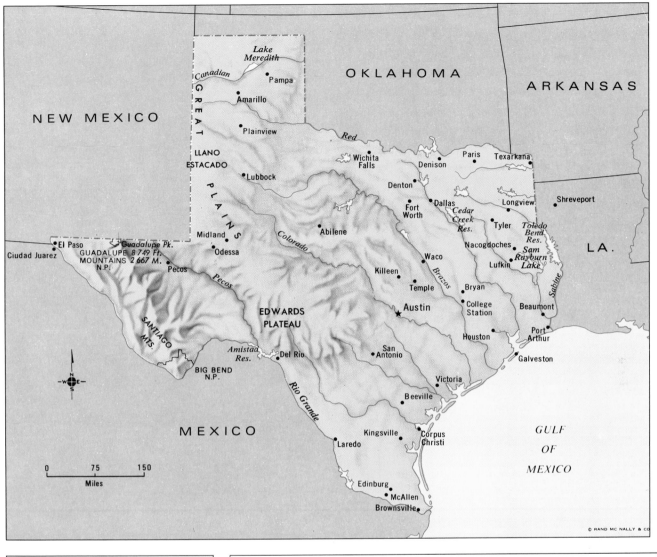

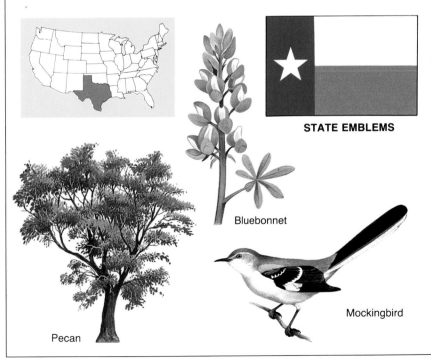

TEXAS

Capital
Austin (518,300 people)

Area
261,914 square miles (678,357 sq. km.) Rank: 2nd

Population
18,153,000 people Rank: 3rd

Statehood
Dec. 29, 1845 (28th state admitted)

Principal rivers
Pecos River, Red River, Rio Grande

Highest point
Guadalupe Peak; 8,749 feet (2,667 m.)

Largest city
Houston (1,703,200 people)

Motto
Friendship

Song
"Texas, Our Texas"

Famous people
Stephen Austin, Sam Houston, Lyndon B. Johnson, Willie Nelson

STATE EMBLEMS

Bluebonnet

Pecan

Mockingbird

Utah

The dry climate and unique geologic history of southeastern Utah have produced many fascinating landforms. The arches, spires, pinnacles, and alcoves of the area combine to form scenery that is considered to be among the most spectacular in North America.

During its geologic history, much of Utah was gradually pushed up from below, causing its rivers to cut deep canyons and expose layers of rock. Additionally, steep mountains were formed. Today, visitors to Utah can see this spectacular scenery in Utah's five national parks, six national monuments, and forty-four state parks.

Although humans have lived in what is now Utah for more than ten thousand years, the region remained unexplored and unsettled by Europeans because of the dry, barren land. The Indians who lived here remained in peace. In the 1840s, a religious group known as Mormons settled in Utah. They came here because they wanted to practice their religion without being bothered by outsiders. Today, about 70 percent of all Utahans are Mormon.

Manufacturing and mining are important in Utah. People mine copper, iron, and lead, and then they turn the ore into usable metals. Most of Utah is very dry. Summers are warm, and winters, cold.

A huge freshwater lake once existed in Utah. Much of the water evaporated, leaving dissolved salts and minerals. The result is the Great Salt Lake, which is eight times saltier than the ocean. Swimmers here find that the heavy salt water makes floating easy.

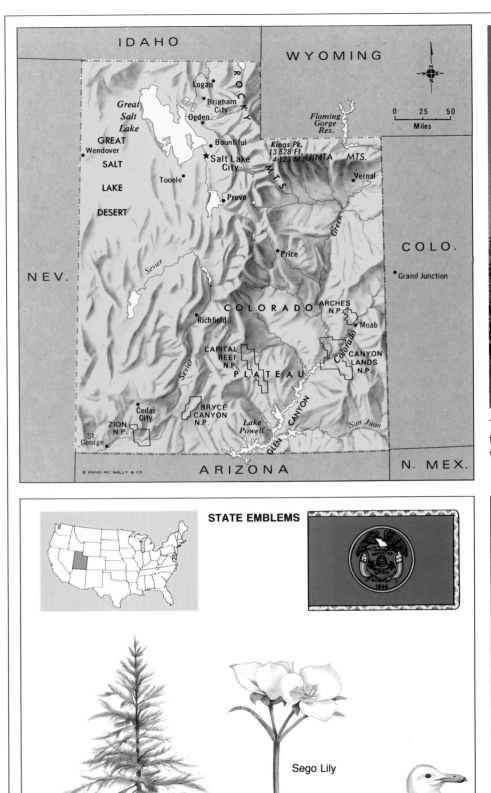

Temple Square in Salt Lake City features the Mormon Temple with its six granite spires.

STATE EMBLEMS

Sego Lily

Blue Spruce

California Gull

UTAH

Capital and largest city
Salt Lake City (169,700 people)

Area
82,168 square miles
(212,815 sq. km.)
Rank: 12th

Population
1,872,600 people
Rank: 34th

Statehood
Jan. 4, 1896 (45th state admitted)

Principal rivers
Colorado River, Green River

Highest point
Kings Peak; 13,528 feet
(4,123 m.)

Motto
Industry

Song
"Utah, We Love Thee"

Famous people
Maude Adams, John Moses Browning, Philo Farnsworth, the Osmond family, Brigham Young

Vermont

In the wake of the American Revolution, Vermont declared itself an independent republic. After a few years, however, it joined the newly formed United States—the first state after the original thirteen colonies to do so. Around the time of the Civil War, Vermont became the first state to ban slavery.

Vermont's forested, mountainous lands are home to the third lowest population of all the states. And, a recent study showed that Vermont was the most rural state in the country. These facts mean Vermont is a state of small towns and farms.

Vermont's low population, mountainous terrain, and climate—which is snowy in winter and cool in summer—combine to make the state a great spot for outdoor activities, such as camping in the summer and skiing in the winter. Especially popular with young people are Vermont's many summer camps.

Making machinery is important in Vermont, and so is dairy farming. Vermonters also produce maple syrup and Christmas trees.

Vermont has no large cities. The town of Topsham, shown here, is situated southeast of Barre and is typical of many communities found in the state. The population of the state is growing, however, and Vermont may become an extension of the eastern megalopolis.

The Appalachian Trail is a mountain path that extends from Maine to Georgia. It runs through fourteen states, including Vermont, for a total of more than 2,050 miles (3,300 kilometers). The trail offers hiking in summer and cross-country skiing in winter.

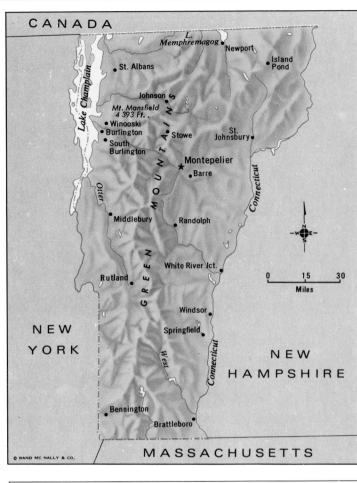

Autumn leaves line the roadside as walkers pass underneath a canopy of fall yellows in Vermont's scenic countryside.

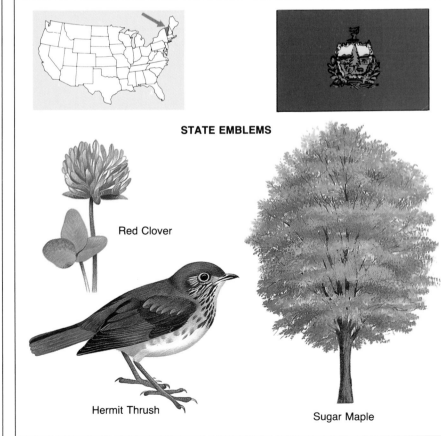

STATE EMBLEMS

Red Clover

Hermit Thrush

Sugar Maple

VERMONT

Capital
Montpelier (8,100 people)

Area
9,249 square miles (23,955 sq. km.) Rank: 43rd

Population
578,600 people Rank: 49th

Statehood
March 4, 1791 (14th state admitted)

Principal river
Connecticut River

Highest point
Mount Mansfield; 4,393 feet (1,339 m.)

Largest city
Burlington (38,400 people)

Motto
Freedom and unity

Song
"Hail, Vermont!"

Famous people
Ethan Allen, Chester Arthur, Calvin Coolidge, George Dewey, Stephen Douglas

Virginia

During most of the 1700s, Williamsburg was the capital of Virginia and one of the most important cities in the colonies. Colonial Williamsburg, in southeastern Virginia, has been recreated and today is one of the leading historic restorations in the United States.

Virginia is a land of history. The first permanent English settlement in the New World, Jamestown, was established in Virginia in 1607. Today, people can visit the reconstructed site. George Washington and Thomas Jefferson, two early presidents of the United States, both lived in Virginia. Their homes, Mount Vernon and Monticello, are open to visitors. During most of the Civil War, Richmond was the capital of the Confederacy, and many major battles were fought in the state. People can visit many sites associated with the War Between the States.

Virginia is right next to Washington, D.C., the center of United States government. Many of the people who live in Virginia work for the government, including the military of the United States. Other Virginians produce chemical and tobacco products, and they raise cattle, poultry, and hogs.

The terrain of Virginia features plains along the coast and mountains inland. Summers are hot, and winters are short with some snowfall.

Virginia is rich in natural beauty as well as history. Shown here are the Blue Ridge Mountains, which are part of the Appalachians. Many people live and farm on the mountains, using the same farming and building methods learned from their grandparents and great-grandparents.

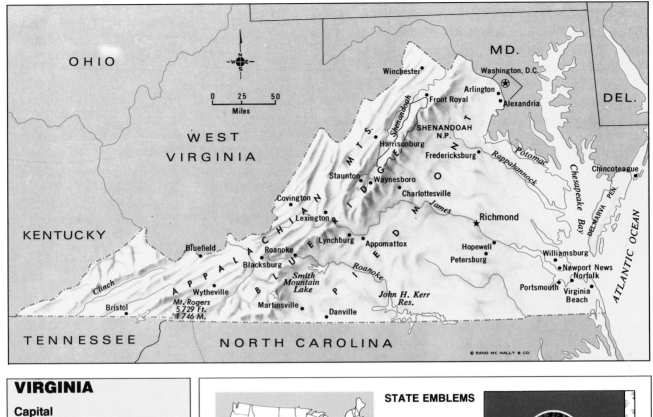

VIRGINIA

Capital
Richmond (200,600 people)

Area
39,598 square miles (102,559 sq. km.) Rank: 37th

Population
6,521,800 people Rank: 12th

Statehood
June 25, 1788 (10th state admitted)

Principal rivers
James River, Potomac River, Rappahannock River

Highest point
Mount Rogers; 5,729 feet (1,746 m.)

Largest city
Virginia Beach (422,700 people)

Motto
Sic semper tyrannis (Thus always to tyrants)

Song
"Carry Me Back to Old Virginia"

Famous people
Ella Fitzgerald, Patrick Henry, Thomas Jefferson, Robert E. Lee, James Madison, James Monroe, George C. Scott, John Tyler, Booker T. Washington, George Washington, Woodrow Wilson

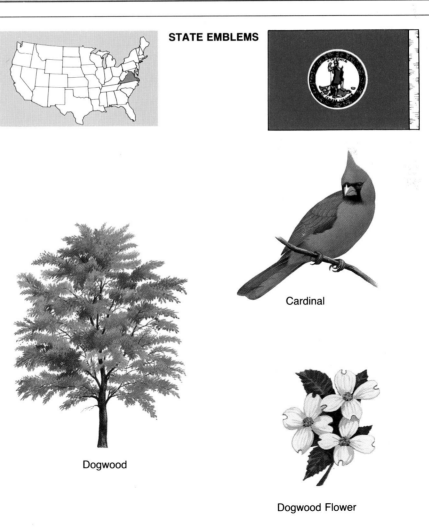

STATE EMBLEMS

Cardinal

Dogwood

Dogwood Flower

Washington

Mount Shuksan, shown here, is one of the peaks of the northern Cascades. The scenic Cascades are a major tourist attraction. Because they block precipitation and are difficult to cross, the Cascades have played a big role in the way the Northwest has developed.

I sland-filled Puget Sound is a place of great natural beauty. With several large ports, it has also become a major shipping center. Here is where most Washingtonians live. Additionally, here is where most of the state's manufacturing is done, with aircraft and missiles important products. Nearby are three national parks and several other wilderness areas. The region surrounding Puget Sound has a moist, mild climate.

East of the Cascades, one finds land of a different character. Here the climate is drier, with moisture-bearing clouds blocked by the high mountain peaks. Far fewer people live here, and those who do tend to be farmers who grow wheat or fruits.

In 1805, the Lewis and Clark Expedition reached Washington by land. As the number of settlers in the area increased, so did conflicts with Indians, who eventually were forced onto reservations. By the late 1800s, lumbering and fishing—especially for salmon—had become important industries in Washington, and they remain so today.

Moving sections of the earth's crust called plates meet in the lands circling the Pacific Ocean. The plates' collisions cause frequent volcanoes and earthquakes, so the region is known as the Ring of Fire. Here is found Mount St. Helens, which erupted violently in 1980.

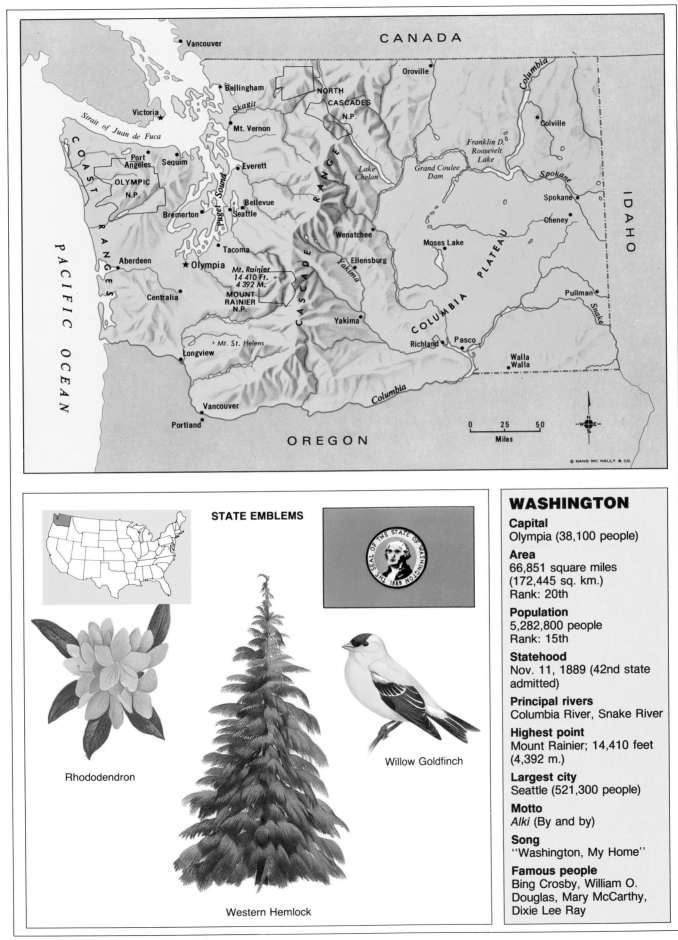

CANADA

Vancouver

Bellingham

Victoria

Strait of Juan de Fuca

Skagit

Oroville

NORTH CASCADES N.P.

Columbia

Colville

Franklin D. Roosevelt Lake

C O A S T   R A N G E S

Port Angeles

Sequim

OLYMPIC N.P.

Mt. Vernon

Everett

Puget Sound

Bellevue

Bremerton

Seattle

Tacoma

Aberdeen

★ Olympia

Centralia

Longview

+ Mt. St. Helens

Vancouver

Portland

OREGON

PACIFIC OCEAN

C A S C A D E   R A N G E

Lake Chelan

Grand Coulee Dam

Wenatchee

Ellensburg

Yakima

Mt. Rainier 14 410 Ft. + 4 392 M.

MOUNT RAINIER N.P.

Yakima

Moses Lake

Richland

Pasco

C O L U M B I A   P L A T E A U

Spokane

Spokane

Cheney

Pullman

Snake

Walla Walla

I D A H O

Columbia

0   25   50
Miles

© RAND MC NALLY & CO.

STATE EMBLEMS

Rhododendron

Western Hemlock

Willow Goldfinch

THE SEAL OF THE STATE OF WASHINGTON 1889

WASHINGTON

Capital
Olympia (38,100 people)

Area
66,851 square miles
(172,445 sq. km.)
Rank: 20th

Population
5,282,800 people
Rank: 15th

Statehood
Nov. 11, 1889 (42nd state admitted)

Principal rivers
Columbia River, Snake River

Highest point
Mount Rainier; 14,410 feet
(4,392 m.)

Largest city
Seattle (521,300 people)

Motto
Alki (By and by)

Song
"Washington, My Home"

Famous people
Bing Crosby, William O. Douglas, Mary McCarthy, Dixie Lee Ray

West Virginia

Under the forests of West Virginia's mountains lie huge mineral deposits. Large-scale mining of these coal, petroleum, and natural gas deposits began after the Civil War. Much coal is dug out of underground mines such as this one, which can be very dangerous.

W est Virginia is a landlocked state; that is, it does not have coastline on any major bodies of water. What it does have, however, is many beautiful mountains. The rugged Appalachian Mountains and the Allegheny Plateau, which is made up of long ridges, cover much of the state. Summers are hot in the valleys and milder in the mountains. Winters are cool.

At the time of the American Revolution, West Virginia was frontier country. West Virginia was part of Virginia at that time, but many West Virginians wanted to form their own state. When the Civil War started in 1861, Virginia joined the Confederacy. But West Virginia broke away from Virginia and joined the Union. West Virginia has been a separate state ever since.

West Virginia's mountainous terrain prevents much agriculture, but some livestock is raised, and hay and fruits are grown. Mining is more important, with coal the most significant mineral by far. West Virginians also manufacture chemicals, iron, and steel.

The Appalachians are the longest mountain system in the eastern United States. They formed a barrier to early settlers, and regions to the west of them remained largely unsettled until after the revolutionary war. Shown here is an area near Spruce Knob, West Virginia.

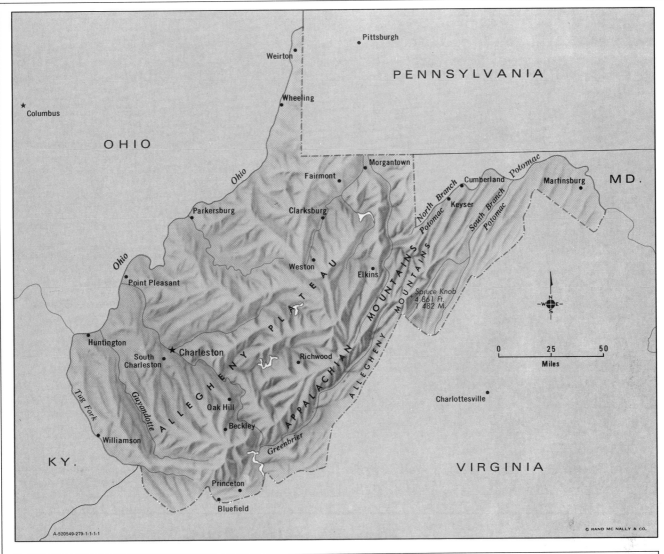

WEST VIRGINIA

Capital and largest city
Charleston (57,000 people)

Area
24,087 square miles (62,381 sq. km.) Rank: 41st

Population
1,816,500 people Rank: 35th

Statehood
June 20, 1863 (35th state admitted)

Principal river
Ohio River

Highest point
Spruce Knob; 4,861 feet (1,482 m.)

Motto
Montani semper liberi
(Mountaineers are always free)

Song
"The West Virginia Hills" and two others

Famous people
Pearl Buck, Thomas "Stonewall" Jackson, Anna Jarvis

STATE EMBLEMS

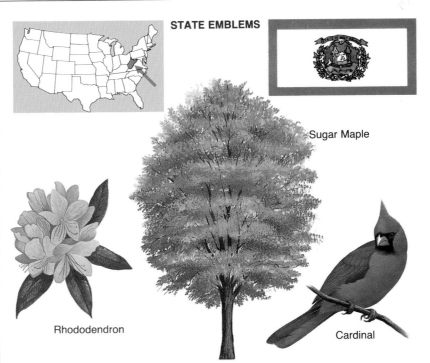

Sugar Maple

Rhododendron

Cardinal

Wisconsin

Wisconsin has placed great importance on conservation. Shown here is the Horicon Marsh Wildlife Refuge in southeastern Wisconsin. Each year, thousands of waterfowl migrate to the refuge to feed and nest. Wisconsin is also home to many other kinds of animals.

To the west and south of the Great Lakes lie fertile plains that were once at the bottom of glacial lakes. This land of gently rolling hills covers much of Wisconsin and other parts of the Midwest. Glaciers also left behind more than eight thousand lakes in the state, many of them in the north. Like the surrounding states, Wisconsin experiences extremes in temperature, with hot summers and cold winters.

Although more people in the state have jobs in manufacturing than in farming, Wisconsin is known for its dairy products. Wisconsin has more dairy cows than any other state. It is the leading producer of milk and cheese in the country. Wisconsinites manufacture machinery, food products, and paper.

Thousands of years ago, after the last glaciers melted, hunters seeking mastodon, giant beaver, and other animals entered what is now Wisconsin. The French were the first Europeans to arrive, in 1634. Many settlers and lead miners came to Wisconsin in the early 1800s.

Wisconsin's quiet beauty can be enjoyed in a number of ways—hiking, camping, and bicycling are just a few. Door Peninsula, which sticks out into Lake Michigan, is a popular resort area that features miles of shoreline and rolling countryside.

Shown here is the capitol building of Wisconsin in Madison.

STATE EMBLEMS

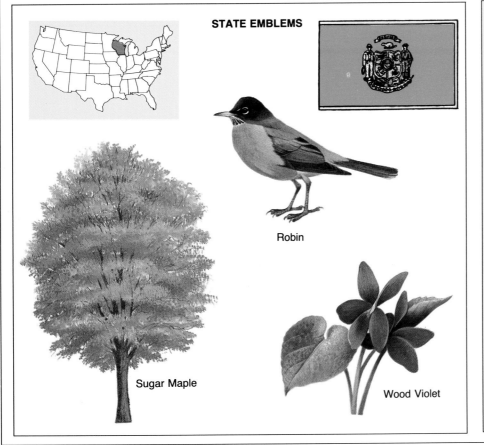

Robin

Sugar Maple

Wood Violet

WISCONSIN

Capital
Madison (195,300 people)

Area
54,314 square miles (140,673 sq. km.) Rank: 25th

Population
5,056,300 people Rank: 18th

Statehood
May 29, 1848 (30th state admitted)

Principal rivers
Mississippi River, Wisconsin River

Highest point
Timms Hill; 1,951 feet (595 m.)

Largest city
Milwaukee (620,400 people)

Motto
Forward

Song
"On, Wisconsin!"

Famous people
Harry Houdini, Robert La Follette, Jacques Marquette, Orson Welles, Thornton Wilder, Frank Lloyd Wright

Wyoming

Many types of animals, both wild and domestic, thrive in Wyoming. The state's wild areas provide refuge for elk, bears, antelopes, mountain lions, lynxes, and bald and golden eagles. Here, horses graze near the mountains of Grand Teton National Park.

Wyoming is one of the last refuges of the American cowboy. Its dude ranches, rodeos, and ranchers on horseback all re-create the atmosphere of the Old West. Tourists coming to Wyoming can glimpse this era as well as view spectacular scenery.

The rugged terrain of the Rocky Mountains in the west and the harsh, dry climate of the Great Plains in the east have done much to keep Wyoming free of settlers. At first, they merely crossed Wyoming as they traveled to more promising lands farther west. When railroads reached Wyoming in 1867, making travel much easier, more people came to Wyoming and to other western regions. But Wyoming still has the lowest population of all the states.

In 1869, Wyoming women became the first in the country to gain the right to vote. The country's first woman governor took office in Wyoming in 1925.

Mining is most important to Wyoming, and oil is the most valuable mineral. Many Wyomingites raise cattle or sheep.

Most of Yellowstone National Park lies in Wyoming. The park is known for its underground hot springs that periodically spurt hot water and steam, or *geysers*. It is also home to a wide variety of wildlife, including moose, bison, coyotes, and bears.

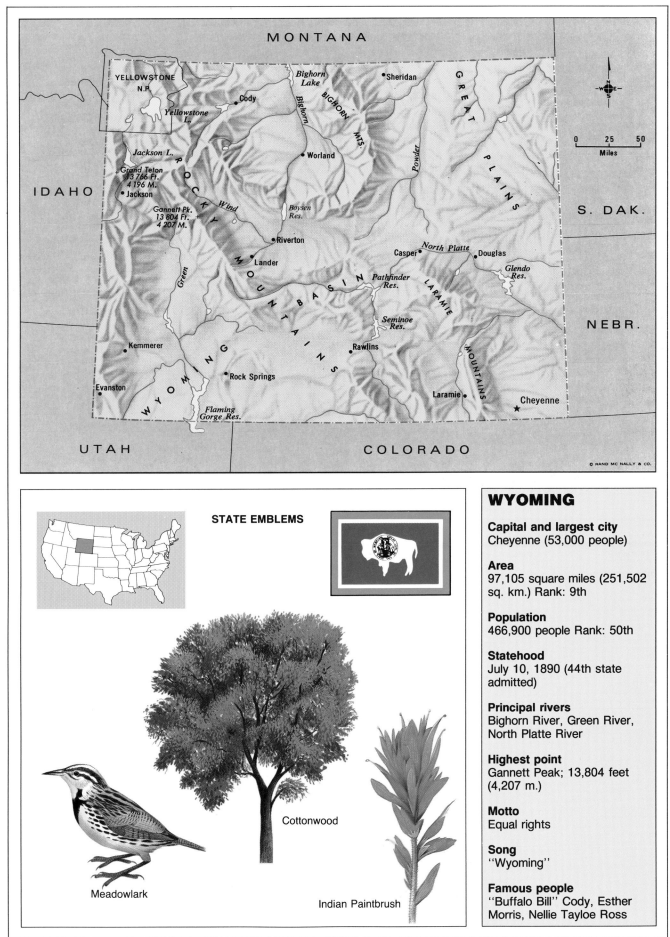

MONTANA

YELLOWSTONE N.P.

Yellowstone L.

Bighorn Lake

Cody

Sheridan

Bighorn

BIGHORN MTS.

GREAT PLAINS

IDAHO

Jackson L.

Grand Teton 13 766 Ft. 4 196 M.

Jackson

Gannett Pk. 13 804 Ft. 4 207 M.

Wind

Worland

Boysen Res.

Powder

R O C K Y   M O U N T A I N S

Green

Riverton

Lander

Casper

North Platte

Douglas

Glendo Res.

S. DAK.

Pathfinder Res.

LARAMIE

NEBR.

Seminoe Res.

Kemmerer

W Y O M I N G   B A S I N

Rawlins

MOUNTAINS

Rock Springs

Laramie

Cheyenne

Evanston

Flaming Gorge Res.

UTAH

COLORADO

© RAND MC NALLY & CO.

0   25   50
Miles

STATE EMBLEMS

Cottonwood

Meadowlark

Indian Paintbrush

WYOMING

Capital and largest city
Cheyenne (53,000 people)

Area
97,105 square miles (251,502 sq. km.) Rank: 9th

Population
466,900 people Rank: 50th

Statehood
July 10, 1890 (44th state admitted)

Principal rivers
Bighorn River, Green River, North Platte River

Highest point
Gannett Peak; 13,804 feet (4,207 m.)

Motto
Equal rights

Song
"Wyoming"

Famous people
"Buffalo Bill" Cody, Esther Morris, Nellie Tayloe Ross

Index of Major Places on the Maps

Place	Page No.	Place	Page No.	Place	Page No.
Acadia National Park, Maine	47	Charleston, West Virginia	105	Grand Canyon National Park, Arizona	15
Adirondack Mountains, New York	73	Charlotte, North Carolina	75	Grand Island, Nebraska	63
Akron, Ohio	79	Chattahoochee River	29	Grand Rapids, Michigan	53
Alabama, state	11	Chattanooga, Tennessee	93	Grand Teton, Wyoming	109
Alaska, state	13	Chesapeake Bay, Maryland, Virginia	49	Great Salt Lake, Utah	97
Albany, New York	73	Cheyenne, Wyoming	109	Great Smoky Mountains National Park, North Carolina, Tennessee	75
Albuquerque, New Mexico	71	Chicago, Illinois	35	Green Bay, Wisconsin	107
Alexandria, Virginia	101	Cincinnati, Ohio	79	Green Mountains, Vermont	99
Allegheny Mountains, West Virginia	105	Cleveland, Ohio	79	Green River, Utah, Wyoming	97
Allentown, Pennsylvania	85	Coast Ranges	19	Greensboro, North Carolina	75
Amarillo, Texas	95	Cod, Cape, Massachusetts	51	Harrisburg, Pennsylvania	85
Anchorage, Alaska	13	Colorado, state	21	Hartford, Connecticut	23
Annapolis, Maryland	49	Colorado River	15	Hawaii, state	31
Ann Arbor, Michigan	53	Colorado River, Texas	95	Hawaii, island, Hawaii	31
Appalachian Mountains	85	Colorado Springs, Colorado	21	Helena, Montana	61
Arizona, state	15	Columbia, South Carolina	89	Honolulu, Hawaii	31
Arkansas, state	17	Columbia River	103	Hood, Mount, Oregon	83
Arkansas River	17	Columbus, Georgia	29	Hot Springs, Arkansas	17
Arlington, Texas	95	Columbus, Ohio	79	Houston, Texas	95
Arlington, Virginia	101	Concord, New Hampshire	67	Hudson River, New York	73
Atlanta, Georgia	29	Connecticut, state	23	Huntington, West Virginia	105
Atlantic City, New Jersey	69	Connecticut River, Connecticut	23	Huntsville, Alabama	11
Augusta, Maine	47	Corpus Christi, Texas	95	Huron, Lake, Michigan	9
Austin, Texas	95	Crater Lake National Park, Oregon	83	Idaho, state	33
Badlands National Park, South Dakota	91	Dallas, Texas	95	Illinois, state	35
Bakersfield, California	19	Dayton, Ohio	79	Illinois River, Illinois	35
Baltimore, Maryland	49	Dearborn, Michigan	53	Independence, Missouri	59
Baton Rouge, Louisiana	45	Death Valley National Monument, California	19	Indiana, state	37
Beaumont, Texas	95	Delaware, state	25	Indianapolis, Indiana	37
Bering Strait, Alaska	13	Delaware River	85	Iowa, state	39
Big Bend National Park, Texas	95	Denver, Colorado	21	Jackson, Mississippi	57
Billings, Montana	61	Des Moines, Iowa	39	Jackson Lake, Wyoming	109
Biloxi, Mississippi	57	Des Moines River, Iowa	39	Jacksonville, Florida	27
Birmingham, Alabama	11	Detroit, Michigan	53	James River, Virginia	101
Bismarck, North Dakota	77	Dover, Delaware	25	Jefferson City, Missouri	59
Bitterroot Range, Idaho, Montana	33	Duluth, Minnesota	55	Jersey City, New Jersey	69
Black Hills, South Dakota	91	Durham, North Carolina	75	Juan de Fuca, Strait of, British Columbia, Washington	103
Block Island, Rhode Island	87	Elizabeth, New Jersey	69	Juneau, Alaska	13
Blue Ridge	101	El Paso, Texas	95	Kansas, state	41
Boise, Idaho	33	Erie, Pennsylvania	85	Kansas City, Kansas	41
Boston, Massachusetts	51	Erie, Lake	9	Kansas City, Missouri	59
Boulder, Colorado	21	Eugene, Oregon	83	Kansas River, Kansas	41
Brazos River, Texas	95	Evansville, Indiana	37	Katahdin, Mount, Maine	47
Bridgeport, Connecticut	23	Fairbanks, Alaska	13	Kauai, island, Hawaii	31
Brownsville, Texas	95	Fargo, North Dakota	77	Kentucky, state	43
Buffalo, New York	73	Finger Lakes, New York	73	Kentucky River, Kentucky	43
Burlington, Vermont	99	Flint, Michigan	53	Knoxville, Tennessee	93
California, state	19	Florida, state	27	Lansing, Michigan	53
Canadian River	81	Fort Lauderdale, Florida	27	Laredo, Texas	95
Canaveral, Cape, Florida	27	Fort Wayne, Indiana	37	Las Vegas, Nevada	65
Carson City, Nevada	65	Fort Worth, Texas	95	Lexington, Kentucky	43
Cascade Range	83	Frankfort, Kentucky	43	Lincoln, Nebraska	63
Casper, Wyoming	109	Fresno, California	19	Little Rock, Arkansas	17
Catskill Mountains, New York	73	Gary, Indiana	37	Long Island, New York	73
Cedar Rapids, Iowa	39	Georgia, state	29	Los Angeles, California	19
Champlain, Lake	99	Glacier National Park, Montana	61	Louisiana, state	45
Charleston, South Carolina	89	Glendale, Arizona	15		

Place	Page No.	Place	Page No.	Place	Page No.
Louisville, Kentucky	43	Ozark Plateau, Arkansas, Missouri	59	South Dakota, state	91
Mackinac, Straits of, Michigan	53	Paterson, New Jersey	69	South Platte River, Colorado, Nebraska	21
Macon, Georgia	29	Pearl Harbor, Hawaii	31	Spokane, Washington	103
Madison, Wisconsin	107	Pearl River, Mississippi	57	Springfield, Illinois	35
Maine, state	47	Pecos River, Texas	95	Springfield, Massachusetts	51
Manchester, New Hampshire	67	Pennsylvania, state	85	Springfield, Missouri	59
Martha's Vineyard, island, Massachusetts	51	Peoria, Illinois	35	Superior, Lake	9
Maryland, state	49	Philadelphia, Pennsylvania	85	Susquehanna River	85
Massachusetts, state	51	Phoenix, Arizona	15	Syracuse, New York	73
Maui, island, Hawaii	31	Pierre, South Dakota	91	Tacoma, Washington	103
Mauna Kea, volcano, Hawaii	31	Pikes Peak, Colorado	21	Tahoe, Lake, California, Nevada	65
Memphis, Tennessee	93	Pittsburgh, Pennsylvania	85	Tallahassee, Florida	27
Mesa, Arizona	15	Platte River, Nebraska	63	Tampa, Florida	27
Metairie, Louisiana	45	Pontchartrain, Lake, Louisiana	45	Tempe, Arizona	15
Miami, Florida	27	Portland, Maine	47	Tennessee, state	93
Michigan, state	53	Portland, Oregon	83	Tennessee River	93
Michigan, Lake	9	Potomac River, Maryland, Virginia	49	Texas, state	95
Milwaukee, Wisconsin	107	Providence, Rhode Island	87	Toledo, Ohio	79
Minneapolis, Minnesota	55	Provo, Utah	97	Tombigbee River, Alabama	11
Minnesota, state	55	Pueblo, Colorado	21	Topeka, Kansas	41
Minnesota River, Minnesota	55	Puget Sound, Washington	103	Trenton, New Jersey	69
Mississippi, state	57	Rainier, Mount, Washington	103	Tucson, Arizona	15
Mississippi River	9	Raleigh, North Carolina	75	Tulsa, Oklahoma	81
Missouri, state	59	Rapid City, South Dakota	91	Tuscaloosa, Alabama	11
Missouri River	9	Red River	45	Utah, state	97
Mitchell, Mount, North Carolina	75	Reno, Nevada	65	Vermont, state	99
Mobile, Alabama	11	Rhode Island, state	87	Virginia, state	101
Mojave Desert, California	19	Richmond, Virginia	101	Virginia Beach, Virginia	101
Montana, state	61	Rio Grande, river	9	Wabash River, Illinois, Indiana	37
Montgomery, Alabama	11	Roanoke, Virginia	101	Warren, Michigan	53
Montpelier, Vermont	99	Rochester, Minnesota	55	Washington, D.C.	49
Nantucket Island, Massachusetts	51	Rochester, New York	73	Washington, state	103
Nashua, New Hampshire	67	Rockford, Illinois	35	Washington, Mount, New Hampshire	67
Nashville, Tennessee	93	Rocky Mountains	21	West Virginia	105
Nebraska, state	63	Sacramento, California	19	Wheeling, West Virginia	105
Nevada, state	65	St. Augustine, Florida	27	Whitney, Mount, California	19
Newark, New Jersey	69	St. Helens, Mount, volcano, Washington	103	Wichita, Kansas	41
New Hampshire, state	67	St. Joseph, Missouri	59	Willamette River, Oregon	83
New Haven, Connecticut	23	St. Lawrence River	73	Wilmington, Delaware	25
New Jersey, state	69	St. Louis, Missouri	59	Winston-Salem, North Carolina	75
New Mexico, state	71	St. Paul, Minnesota	55	Wisconsin, state	107
New Orleans, Louisiana	45	St. Petersburg, Florida	27	Wisconsin River, Wisconsin	107
Newport News, Virginia	101	Salem, Oregon	83	Worcester, Massachusetts	51
New York, New York	73	Salt Lake City, Utah	97	Wyoming, state	109
New York, state	73	San Antonio, Texas	95	Yazoo River, Mississippi	57
Niagara Falls, New York	73	San Bernardino, California	19	Yellowstone Lake, Wyoming	109
Norfolk, Virginia	101	San Diego, California	19	Yellowstone National Park, Wyoming	109
North Carolina, state	75	San Francisco, California	19	Yellowstone River, Montana	61
North Dakota, state	77	San Jose, California	19	Yonkers, New York	73
North Platte River, Nebraska, Wyoming	109	Santa Fe, New Mexico	71	Yosemite National Park, California	19
Oahu, island, Hawaii	31	Sault Ste. Marie, Michigan	53	Youngstown, Ohio	79
Oakland, California	19	Savannah, Georgia	29	Yukon River, Alaska, Yukon	13
Ogden, Utah	97	Savannah River, Georgia, South Carolina	29		
Ohio, state	79	Scottsdale, Arizona	15		
Ohio River	9	Seattle, Washington	103		
Okeechobee, Lake, Florida	27	Selma, Alabama	11		
Oklahoma, state	81	Shreveport, Louisiana	45		
Oklahoma City, Oklahoma	81	Sierra Nevada, mountains, California	19		
Olympia, Washington	103	Sioux Falls, South Dakota	91		
Omaha, Nebraska	63	Snake River	33		
Ontario, Lake	9	South Bend, Indiana	37		
Oregon, state	83	South Carolina, state	89		
Orlando, Florida	27				